P9-DUF-785

THE SIGNED ENGLISH STARTER

HARRY BORNSTEIN AND KAREN L. SAULNIER

Illustrated by Ralph R. Miller, Sr.

The Signed English Series

CLERC BOOKS
Gallaudet University Press
Washington, D.C.

CLERC BOOKS
An imprint of Gallaudet University Press
Washington, DC 20002

© 1984 by Gallaudet University. All rights reserved.
Fifth printing, 1995
Printed in the United States of America

Library of Congress Cataloging in Publication Data

Bornstein, Harry.
The signed English starter.

(The signed English series)
Includes index.
1. Sign language—Study and teaching. 2. Deaf—
Education—English language. I. Saulnier, Karen Luczak.
II. Miller, Ralph R.   III. Title.   IV. Series.
HV2474.B67 1984 419 84-4042
ISBN 0-913580-82-1

Gallaudet University is an equal opportunity employer/educational institution.
Programs and services offered by Gallaudet University receive substantial
financial support from the U.S. Department of Education.

CONTENTS

CONTENTS

PREFACE

For more than a decade we have tried to make Signed English a more complete and accurate parallel to English. Our principal tools have been dictionaries. Our first was *The Basic Preschool Signed English Dictionary.* This was replaced by *The Signed English Dictionary: For Preschool and Elementary Levels* which, in turn, has been replaced by *The Comprehensive Signed English Dictionary.* Each dictionary is considerably larger than its predecessor and provides additional information on the optimal use of Signed English.

At the same time, we have been concerned that the Signed English system be relatively easy to learn. To this end, we have produced 12 beginning books, 18 growing-up books and stories, and 20 books of more advanced stories and poems. In addition we have prepared a song book with an accompanying record, and three decorative posters.

Of particular significance are our special purpose books, each directed at a selected audience. The first, *Signed English for the Classroom,* was designed for teachers, classroom aides, and teachers-in-training. The second, *Signed English for the Residence Hall,* was made for dormitory counselors and other campus personnel such as secretaries, maintenance workers, nurses, doctors, and administrators.

Our final special purpose book is the one you are holding: *The Signed English Starter.* It is designed to be a first course in Signed English for home or class study. It provides a basic, functional sign vocabulary, a systematic progression in the use of the 14 sign markers, discussion of the unique features of a manual English sign system, a glossary of terms, and a page of exercises following each of the 12 chapters in the book. It will function as a comfortable and reasonable start to learning Signed English.

Finally, we would like to take this opportunity to thank all who have contributed in any way to this book as well as all deaf persons, parents, and teachers who have encouraged and supported us in the past. The work of the following artists is used throughout the book: Linda C. Tom, Nancy L. Lundborg, Ann Silver, and Jack L. Fennell.

INTRODUCTION

As its name suggests *The Signed English Starter* is designed
to start you and your child or student on the way to profi-
ciency in Signed English. For those of you who work with or
teach very limited learners, this book may be the whole jour-
ney. Its contents may be enough, indeed more than enough,
for your needs. However, those of you who deal with other-
wise unimpaired deaf children or adults will surely need to
continue on to the other resources or tools that are available
in the Signed English series. In either case, this book is a
"first course" for those people, especially parents, who need
to teach and/or interact with hearing-impaired people in an
English mode.

HOW DEAF CHILDREN LEARN ENGLISH

Children learn English from others. They learn from what
they hear and see. If their hearing is impaired, they will have
to depend more on what they see than the hearing child.
Therefore, a hearing-impaired child can learn English
through a combination of (a) hearing some of the spoken
words (with or without the aid of amplification), (b) reading
lips, and/or (c) seeing some manual language symbols.
Accordingly, Signed English is a manual English system
designed to be used with speech. It is a semantic system in
which the signs, although largely taken from American Sign
Language (ASL), represent the meanings of words found in
standard English dictionaries. They do not represent the
spelling or the sound of those words. Although Signed English is by far the simplest manual English system in general
use, it is not easy to learn nor is it necessarily the most "comfortable" way to communicate manually. For that matter,
standard English is not necessarily the most comfortable way
to speak; yet it is an essential tool for educational and eco-
nomic achievement and advancement.

You may wonder why a manual English system is more useful for teaching and learning English than American Sign
Language. These are the reasons. American Sign Language
has a different structure or syntax than English. Therefore,
for all practical purposes, it is not possible to speak syntacti-
cally correct English sentences and use ASL at the same

time. Further, since only about three percent of hearing-impaired children have two hearing-impaired parents, the language of the home is most often English. It is easier for parents to learn a manual English system than it is to learn ASL. Finally, ASL has no widely accepted writing system. Manual English should make for an easier transition to reading and writing English.

THE PURPOSE OF SIGNED ENGLISH

Signed English serves two basic purposes. First, it is a model of the English language. Second, it is used to communicate information between people. When it first becomes known that the child has a hearing impairment, it is very important that the adult serve as a language model while communicating information. Later, when the child is older and has mastered language patterns, it is usually acceptable to concentrate on exchanging information. At that time the language modeling function becomes less important. In educational settings, it is probably always desirable for the teacher to remain a model. Let us talk further about some of the implications of the two basic purposes of Signed English.

Because Signed English should be used with speech, the signs are not the only source of information. Depending upon the degree of hearing loss and the quality of amplification used, hearing-impaired children also receive some information from the actual sounds of speech. Further, they receive some information from the shape of the lips as the speaker forms his or her words. Indeed, they also receive information from the eyes, eyebrows, and a host of other small clues. The point being made is a simple one: A manual English system is a second, parallel and redundant model of English for the hearing-impaired child. It need not, and indeed cannot, perfectly represent English. This would make Signed English so complex as to be virtually unlearnable. Using your hands to parallel your speech in an English model is very difficult if you try to mirror all of the features of the language at secondary or higher education levels. At that point in his or her education, a student should have mastery over many features of English. Under those circumstances it may not be necessary to use all of the sign markers and function words all of the time. The student can unconsciously fill in what you omit from your hands and receive the information from context and/or lip movements. Generally speaking, however, when you reach the stage where you might be making such adjustments, you will have advanced beyond this first course.

THE ORGANIZATION OF THIS BOOK

Signed English uses two kinds of gestures or signs: sign words and sign markers. The sign words, or vocabulary, comprise the greatest portion of this book and are arranged within topical chapters for easier learning. In preparing this book we explored a full range of vocabulary lists that were suggested as useful or highly functional for young children without intellectual impairment. We also examined vocabulary lists for the full age range of those children who suffer from severe intellectual, emotional, or physical impairment. As a consequence, we selected approximately 900 sign words to be included in this book. Most of the signs are borrowed from American Sign Language. Where two signs exist for a given word, we chose the simplest to execute. Other signs are modifications of ASL signs. We think this group of signs will meet most of your basic needs.

Beyond these sign words, other vocabulary you may need for daily conversation will be used so infrequently it is easier to fingerspell them than to learn other existing or invented signs. Similarly, the rather large group of infrequently used English affixes (prefixes and suffixes) should also be spelled. When an affix is fingerspelled, fingerspell the entire word.

In order to use the sign vocabulary in the same order as words are used in an English sentence, sign markers are used to present a complete model of English grammar. A description of the 14 sign markers in the Signed English system is given on pages xii–xiii and at the beginning of some chapters. These markers, which add to or change the meaning of the basic word, are the ones most frequently used in English, but even among them there is wide variation in frequency of use. For example, the plurals and the past are much more frequently used than the comparative marker. Consequently, if you use all 14 markers, you can expect that a child will learn the plurals and the past much earlier than the comparative. However, a child will not learn any of the affixes without regular, consistent exposure to them. We urge you, therefore, to learn and use the entire set of 14 markers.

If you have reason to believe that a child will be a very limited learner because of some severe learning problem such as retardation or autism, then it may be advisable to use fewer markers or none at all. Use simple, uninflected sentences relating to the immediate experiences of the child. In effect, you will be providing a limited language model because of your belief that the child or adult is only capable of learning and managing very basic communication needs. However, judgments of limited capability have profound effects and should not be made lightly.

In addition to sign words and sign markers, basic Signed English principles, the third kind of information given in this book, are presented at the beginning of some chapters.

You will find practice material at the end of each chapter. The material moves in complexity from short phrases and simple sentences in the earlier chapters to paragraphs of connected discourse in the final chapters. The words that are hyphenated letter by letter (e.g., m-o-t-h-e-r) are words without signs or whose signs will be presented later in the book. These words are to be fingerspelled. Mastery of the practice material will improve one's signing and fingerspelling skills.

SIGN MARKERS

Signed English uses two kinds of gestures or signs: sign words and sign markers. Each sign word stands for one English word, such as *mother, shoe, horse,* etc. These sign words should be signed in the same order as words are used in an English sentence.

The sign markers should be used when you wish to change the form and the meaning of some words in a sentence. This includes such things as changes in number, possession, degree, verb tense, etc. We recommend that you use the 14 sign markers pictured here.

All but one of these markers are signed after the basic sign word. The marker that stands for "opposite of" is the only marker that is signed before the sign word.

In Signed English you use either a sign word alone or a sign word and one sign marker to represent a given English word. When this does not adequately represent the word you have in mind, use the manual alphabet and fingerspell the word.

If you use these markers properly, you will provide a better and more complete model of English.

regular plural nouns: -s
bears, houses

irregular plural nouns:
(sign the word twice)
children, sheep, mice

regular past verbs: -ed
talked, wanted,
learned

irregular past verbs:
(sweep RH open B, tips
out, to the right) saw,
heard, blew

3rd person singular: -s
walk*s*, eat*s*, sing*s*

possessive: -'s
cat*'s*, daddy*'s*, chair*'s*

verb form: -ing
climb*ing*, play*ing*,
runn*ing*

participle :
fall*en*, go*ne*, grow*n*

adjective: -y
sleep*y*, sunn*y*,
cloud*y*

adverb: -ly
beautiful*ly*, happi*ly*,
nice*ly*

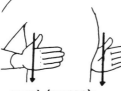

agent (person):
(sign made near the
body) teach*er*, act*or*,
art*ist*

agent (thing):
(sign made away from
the body) wash*er*, dry*er*,
plant*er*

comparative: -er
small*er*, fast*er*,
long*er*

superlative: -est
small*est*, fast*est*,
long*est*

opposite of: un-
(made before the sign
word, as a prefix)
*un*happy, *un*important

AMERICAN MANUAL ALPHABET

Fingerspelling is an important part of Signed English. It fills in the "sign gaps" in your sentences if you do not know the sign for a particular word.

Fingerspelling is a letter-by-letter manual representation of English words. Each letter of the alphabet is represented by a specific handshape. Form the letters with your hand held up comfortably about chest level, the palm facing outward, i.e., toward your audience.

Make your letters in a smooth, clear manner. Pause slightly between words but do not drop your hand. Avoid bouncing or pushing letters forward in an attempt to be clear.

Do not move your hand position while fingerspelling. However, when fingerspelling a word that contains a double letter (e.g., *soon, hall*) you may move your hand slightly to the right when forming the second letter.

Remember always to say words, not individual letters, while signing and fingerspelling words. Do not let your hands obscure your lip movements.

Most formal names for people, places, and things, as well as addresses, are fingerspelled.

NAME SIGNS

Although names for people can always be fingerspelled, it is often convenient and much more personal to devise a "name sign," especially for family members and friends.

The following are some of the most common approaches to developing name signs.

Using English Initials (Initialization)
The first letter of the person's first (or sometimes last) name is placed on the body in a clearly seen location above the waist. Common locations are on the center of the chest (fig. 1), on the chest above the heart (fig. 2), along the left arm (fig. 3), on the elbow (fig. 4), and on the wrist (fig. 5).

Manual letters may also be placed so that they indicate the sex of the person, i.e., at the forehead for males and at the chin for females. For example, W for Walter might be placed at the forehead level (fig. 6), while T for Tamara would be placed at the chin level (fig. 7).

Oftentimes the first letter of the person's name is placed in the fingerspelling position and shaken gently from side to side (fig. 8).

Emphasizing Important Characteristics
The location of the initial(s) or name sign is often coupled with an outstanding feature of a person. The initial letter of a name may be placed at eye level for a person who wears eyeglasses (fig. 9), or at the middle of the chest for a man who always wears a tie (fig. 10). Some examples of this type of name sign are the L at the top of the head for Abraham Lincoln's hat (fig. 11), and the S zigzagging down the chest for the design on Superman's outfit (fig. 12).

Please note that any initials placed on the nose generally have a negative meaning. To avoid creating a name sign which may be confused with an already existing sign or which may be derogatory in nature, discuss your choice with a deaf adult or your sign language teacher.

1. A for Aimee
in center of chest

2. B for Bob
on chest above heart

3. D for Dan
along left arm

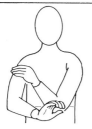

4. C for Carol
on elbow

5. F for Frank
on wrist

6. W for Walter
at forehead

7. T for Tamara
at chin level

8. E for Elizabeth
shake letter sign

9. R for Ruth
who wears glasses

10. P for Peter
who wears ties

11. L for Lincoln

12. S for Superman

NUMBERS

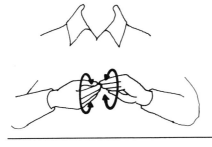

number
Flat O shape both hands, left palm in, right down, tips touching. Reverse positions.

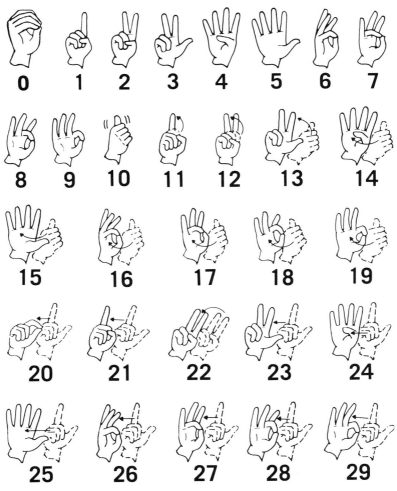

30–99

Thirty through ninety-nine:
Sign by forming the two figures that comprise the number.

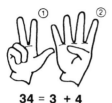

34 = 3 + 4   60 = 6 + 0

100

One hundred:
Form the number 1, then C with right hand.

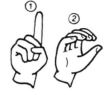

1,000

One thousand:
Form the number 1 with RH. Then place tips of right M in left palm.

1,000,000

One million:
Form the number 1 with RH. Then place tips of right M in left palm. Bounce tips forward once (twice for billion).

Ordinal Numbers

Sign 1st through 9th by signing the number (palm out) then twisting to palm in.

8th

Fractions

Sign the numerator then lower hand slightly and sign the denominator.

1/4   3/8

KEY to WORD DESCRIPTIONS

In order to use this book easily and effectively, you should be familiar with the names of your fingers, the manual alphabet, the signs for the numbers one through ten, and certain hand-shapes that are frequently used when making the base signs.

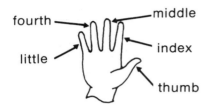

- **RH** = **right hand**
- **LH** = **left hand**

ILLUSTRATIONS

first position of right hand

arrow showing direction of movement

final position of right hand

HANDSHAPES

Sample letter shape A. See complete alphabet on page xiv.

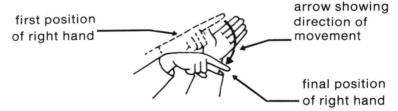

Sample number shape 1. See numbers 1–29 on page xviii.

open B　　**bent B**　　**bent V**　　**claw shape**　　**flat O**

KEY to ARROWS

The dotted line shows the starting point of a sign. The directional arrow shows the movement toward the solid-line (or final) hand position.

Arrows indicate single, double, or repeated movement as described below:

single movement, once toward point

double movement, twice toward point

repeated movement, back and forth

repeated movement, forward, back, and forward

right arc (directions are from the perspective of the signer in the drawings)

left arc

clockwise, counterclockwise

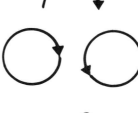

motion markers indicate a slight wiggling movement

1.
PEOPLE
and
PRONOUNS

REGULAR PLURAL NOUNS

Add the regular plural marker to most nouns to indicate more than one person or thing.

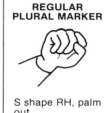

REGULAR PLURAL MARKER

S shape RH, palm out.

baby + regular plural marker = **babies**

IRREGULAR PLURAL NOUNS

Some plural nouns do not end in *s*. Use the irregular plural marker for these words.

IRREGULAR PLURAL MARKER

mice

Make the base sign two or more times.

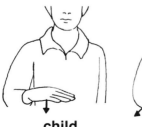 

child   **children**

PEOPLE AND OCCUPATIONS

Some signs are used alone to stand for people or occupations.

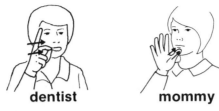

dentist   **mommy**

Other base signs must be used with the agent (person) marker to represent people or occupations.

AGENT (PERSON) MARKER
Move both open B hands, tips out, down close to sides of body.

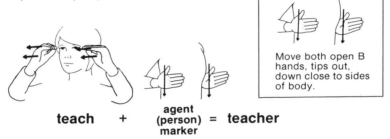

teach   +   **agent (person) marker**   =   **teacher**

The agent (person) marker is also used for some occupations ending in -or (e.g., *actor*) and -ist (e.g., *artist*). You must memorize which base signs are used alone and which signs must be used with the agent (person) marker.

PRONOUNS ENDING IN -S

To form pronouns ending in -s, first sign the base pronoun. Then form an S shape RH and push it forward slightly.

yours   **hers**   **theirs**

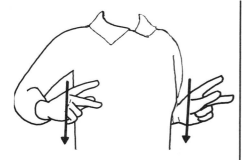

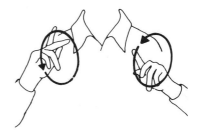

person

P shape both hands, middle finger-tips out. Place wrists against sides of body then move down.

people

P shape both hands, palms out. Move up and down alternately in circular motion.

family

F shape both hands, palms out, thumbs and index fingers touching. Draw apart and around until little fingers touch.

friend

Hook right X over left X which is turned up, then reverse.

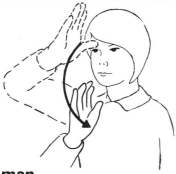

man

RH open B palm left. Touch thumb to forehead then arc down to the chest.

woman

Brush thumb of A shape RH down chin then place on chest, opening into open B shape.

3

parent
P shape RH. Place middle fingertip on right side of forehead then
on chin.

baby
Place right arm in left arm at waist
and move as if rocking a baby.

boy
Snap flat O at forehead twice,
indicating brim of cap.

girl
A shape RH. Place thumb on right
cheek and move down jaw line.

child
Lower RH, palm down, indicating
height of child.

children
RH open B palm down. Bounce
down two or three times to the
right.

mommy (mama)
Five shape RH palm left, tips up.
Tap chin with thumb twice.

daddy
Five shape RH palm left, tips up.
Tap forehead with thumb twice.

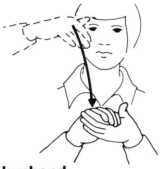

husband
Place thumb of curved open B at
right temple. Move down and clasp
LH which is held palm up.

wife
Cupped shape LH palm up. Move
thumb of right A down right cheek
then clasp hands together.

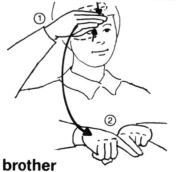

brother
Snap flat O at forehead then
tap index fingers of 1 shapes,
palms down, together.

sister
One shape LH palm down, tip out.
Place right thumb on right cheek.
Change to 1 shape RH and place
index fingers together.

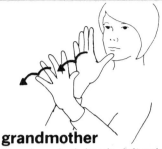

grandmother

Five shape both hands, left palm right, right palm left. Place right thumb on chin and left thumb on edge of RH. Move out in two short jumps. (Sometimes made with RH only.)

grandfather

Five shape both hands, left palm right, right palm left. Place right thumb on forehead and left thumb on edge of RH. Move out in two short jumps. (Sometimes made with RH only.)

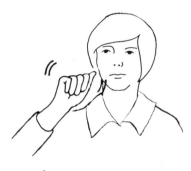

aunt

A shape RH. Wiggle at side of right cheek.

uncle

U shape RH. Wiggle at right temple.

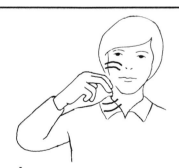

niece

Shake right N at right jawline.

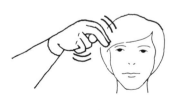

nephew

Shake right N at right temple.

boss
B shape RH, tips slanted left. Tap left upper chest twice.

police
Tap right C just below left shoulder (indicating badge).

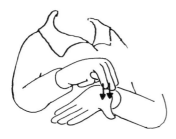

doctor
LH open B palm up, tips out. Tap left wrist with tips of right M.

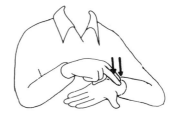

nurse
LH open B palm up. Tap left wrist twice with tips of right N.

dentist
Tap right side of mouth with middle finger and thumb of right D.

soldier
S shape both hands, palms in. Place right S on left upper chest and left S just underneath as if holding a rifle.

I
I shape RH palm left. Place thumb side on chest.

me
Touch chest with index finger.

my
Place palm on chest.

mine
Slap chest twice with palm of right open B.

myself
A shape RH, palm twisted right. Tap chest with knuckles twice.

it
LH open B tips out. Place tip of right little finger in palm of LH.

he
E shape RH palm left. Place on right temple, then move out slightly toward right.

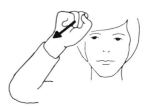

his
Place right S just above right eye. Move out slightly toward right.

him
Place fingertips of right M just above right eye. Move out slightly toward right.

she
E shape RH knuckles left. Place on right cheek then move forward.

her
R shape RH. Place on right cheek then move out slightly to the right.

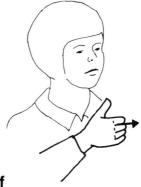

self
A shape RH palm left, thumb up. Move forward and out.

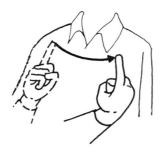

we
Touch right index finger to right side of chest then arc to left.

us
U shape RH. Place tips on right side of chest then arc over to left side.

our
Place thumb of cupped RH just under right shoulder. Arc to left, ending with little finger resting just below left shoulder.

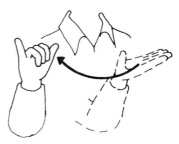

they
RH open B palm up, tips out. Slide from left to right, twisting into Y shape palm out.

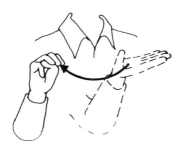

them
RH open B palm up, tips out. Slide from left to right, twisting to M shape RH.

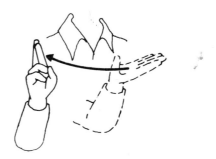

their
RH open B palm up, tips out. Slide from left to right, twisting to R shape RH palm out.

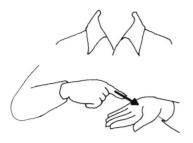

this
LH open B palm up, tips out. Tap LH with right index finger.

that
Place knuckles of right Y on up-turned left palm.

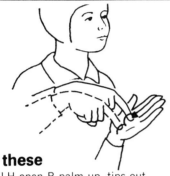

these
LH open B palm up, tips out. Bounce right index tip forward in left palm two or three times.

those
LH open B palm up, tips out. Tap knuckles of right Y on base of left palm, then on fingers.

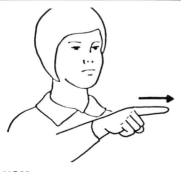

you
Point index finger at person being addressed.

your
Push palm forward toward person being addressed.

Practice signing and saying the following phrases and short sentences. Fingerspell all words hyphenated letter by letter (e.g., m-o-t-h-e-r).

1. his wife
2. her husband
3. my parents
4. their grandmother
5. our family
6. boys a-n-d girls
7. that soldier
8. these children
9. this nurse
10. himself
11. yourself
12. my boss
13. those men
14. That i-s hers.
15. This i-s yours.
16. Those a-r-e mine.
17. our friends
18. these women
19. her brother a-n-d sister
20. his uncle a-n-d aunt
21. That i-s my baby.
22. their niece
23. your nephews
24. I h-u-r-t myself.
25. policemen

2.
THINGS

POSSESSIVES

To show possession add the possessive marker (-'s) to the base sign.

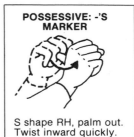

POSSESSIVE: -'S MARKER

S shape RH, palm out. Twist inward quickly.

daddy + **possessive -'s marker** + **book = daddy's book**

AGENT (THING) MARKER

To form certain words that end in -*er,* add the agent (thing) marker after the base sign.

AGENT (THING) MARKER

Move both open B hands, tips out, down in front of body.

wash + **agent (thing) marker** = **washer (machine)**

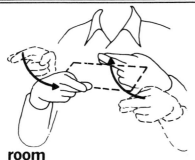

room

R shape both hands, tips out. Turn right R left and left R right to form box shape.

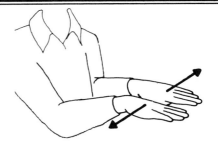

floor

B shape both hands, palms down, tips out, index fingers touching. Move apart.

wall

W shape both hands, palms in, held close together. Move hands apart then back, outlining shape of wall.

window

Open B both hands, palms in, tips opposite. Place right little finger on left index. Move up then down.

door

B shape both hands, palms out slightly, tips a little up. Place index fingers together then turn RH to the right, ending with palm up. Return to starting position.

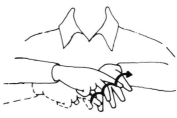

stair

Five shape LH palm down, tips out. "Walk" over back of left fingers with right middle and index fingers.

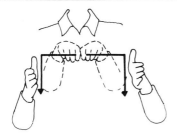

table
Open B shape both hands, palms down, tips out. Draw apart and down, outlining shape of table. (Sometimes made with T hand-shapes.)

lamp
RH flat O palm down. Rest right elbow in left palm. Drop right flat O into 5 shape, palm down.

chair
C shape LH palm right. Hang right N over left thumb.

couch
C shape both hands, left palm out, right palm left. Hook right C over thumb of left C.

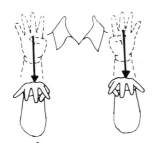

curtain
Four shape both hands. Drop forward and down, ending with palms down.

rug
LH open B palm down, tips out. R shape RH palm down, tips left. Place RH on left wrist and slide to fingertips.

mirror
RH open B palm in. Hold before face and twist slightly to the right. Repeat motion.

picture
LH open B palm right, tips up. Place thumb and index finger of right C against right eye then move down to left palm.

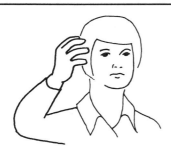

radio
Place cupped right hand over right ear.

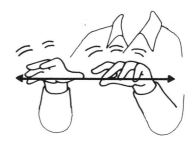

piano
Mime playing piano.

telephone
Y shape RH. Place thumb on ear and little finger on mouth.

television
Fingerspell T-V in quick succession as if one movement.

bed
Place right palm on right cheek and tilt head slightly.

blanket
B shape both hands, palms down, tips facing. Move toward chest, as if pulling blanket up to neck.

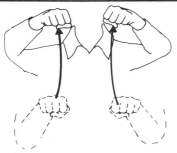

sheet
S shape both hands, knuckles down. Draw up from waist to shoulders, as if pulling up sheet.

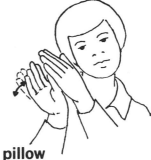

pillow
Place back of left open B at right side of head. Tilt head to right and mime patting underside of pillow with tips of cupped RH.

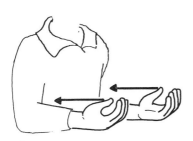

drawer
Hold cupped hands in front of body palms up, then draw back as if pulling drawer open.

shelf
Open B both hands held high, palms down, tips out. Hold together then move apart in straight line.

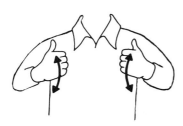

bath
A shape both hands, knuckles in, thumbs up. Make scrubbing motion on chest.

toilet
Shake right T from left to right several times.

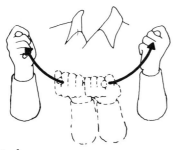

tub
T shape both hands, palms up, little fingers touching. Move apart and up, outlining shape of tub.

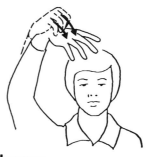

shower
S shape RH palm down. Hold above head and open into 5 shape. Repeat motion.

shampoo
Claw shape both hands. Place tips on head and rub back and forth, as if shampooing hair.

soap
Open B both hands, left palm up, tips out; right palm in, tips down. Draw right fingers backward across left palm ending in A shape.

toothbrush
Rub edge of right index finger back and forth over teeth.

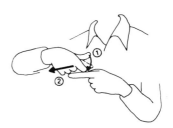

toothpaste
Mime spreading paste on toothbrush.

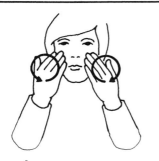

towel
Open B both hands, palms facing, tips up. Circle palms on cheeks.

laundry
L shape both hands, left palm up, tips slanted right; right palm down, tips slanted left. Twist hands back and forth.

broom
S shape both hands. Mime holding broom and sweeping.

vacuum cleaner
V shape RH palm down, tips out. Move back and forth, as if vacuuming.

kitchen
K shape RH. Shake back and forth.

cabinet
Place thumbs and index tips of both hands together. Mime opening up cabinet doors.

refrigerator
R shape both hands, palms facing, tips out. Shake back and forth in "shivering" motion.

oven
LH open B palm down, tips
O shape RH palm and tips
Slide RH under left open B

stove
S shape RH palm in. Place at mouth then twist wrist quickly so that palm faces down.

sink
C shape LH palm and tips right, little finger side down. S shape RH. Place right arm in left C and slowly wiggle down (sink out of sight).

box
Open B both hands, palms facing, thumbs up. Turn LH right and RH left to form shape of box.

bag
S shape LH knuckles down. Place index finger of right B on left S and circle under LH.

basket
Place index finger of right B under left wrist and arc to elbow, ending with little finger side touching.

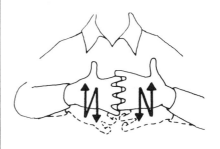

machine
Interlock fingers, palms in, and move up and down.

battery
B shape LH. Strike left index finger with knuckle of right index finger twice.

candle
Five shape RH. Place tip of left index finger on right wrist. Wiggle fingers of RH.

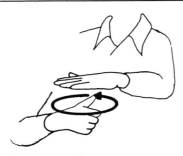

basement
LH open B palm down, tips right. Circle right A, thumb extended, under right B counterclockwise.

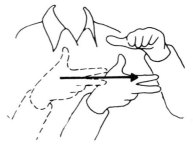

garage
LH open B palm down, tips out. Slide right 3 (palm in) under left hand.

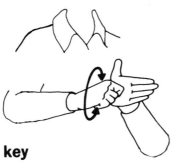

key
LH open B palm right, tips out. Twist knuckle of right index in left palm.

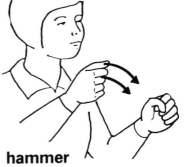

hammer
S shape LH knuckles right. A shape RH. Move right A toward left S as if hitting nail.

camera
Mime holding camera in front of face and clicking shutter.

thing
RH open B palm up, tips out. Move out and to the right in small bouncing movements.

mail
Place thumb of right A on mouth. Change to M shape and place tips in upturned left palm.

magazine
LH open B palm right, tips out. Grasp bottom of LH with right index and thumb and slide RH forward.

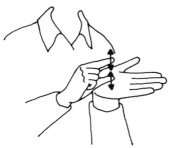

newspaper
LH open B palm up, tips out. Place thumb of right G in left palm then snap tips together two or three times.

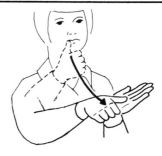

letter (mail)
Place thumb of right A on mouth and then on upturned left palm.

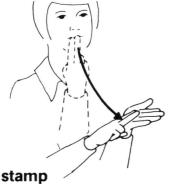

stamp
LH open B palm up, tips out. Place tips of right H on lips then move down and place in left palm.

string
S shape LH palm out. Place tip of right I on left S then shake away to the right.

light (noun)
Right flat O palm down. Hold up at right side then drop fingers into 5 shape palm down.

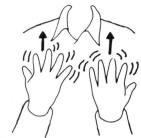

fire
Curved 5 shape both hands, palms in. Move up, fluttering fingers.

cigarette
Tap left index with right index and little finger several times.

tissue
LH open B palm up, tips out. T shape RH palm down, knuckles left. Brush base of right T across base of left palm twice.

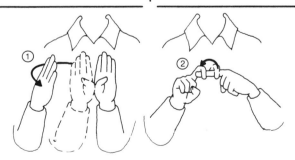

closet
B shape both hands, index fingers touching. Turn RH to right, then hook right index over base of left and move forward.

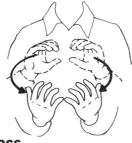

class

C shape both hands held close together. Draw apart and around to front ending in 5 shapes, little fingers touching.

gym (class)

A shape both hands, knuckles facing. Hold above shoulders and move forward in circular movements. (Sometimes made with G shapes.)

cafeteria

Place tips of flat O on mouth. Then form A shapes both hands, palms facing, and move from right to left.

meeting (noun)

Five shape both hands, palms facing, tips up. Bring tips together, forming flat O shapes.

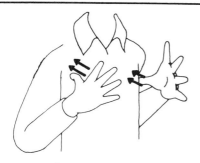

vacation

Five shape both hands, palms facing, tips out. Tap upper chest with thumbs several times.

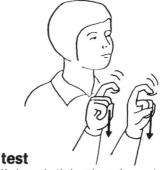

test

X shape both hands, palms out. Crook and uncrook index fingers several times while moving hands downward.

book
Palms together thumbs up. Open as if opening book.

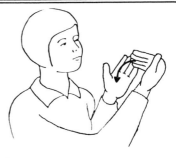

lesson
Open B both hands, RH fingers bent. Place little finger side of RH on fingertips, then heel, of left palm.

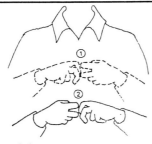

problem
Bent V shapes both hands, right palm down, left palm in. Place knuckles together then twist in opposite directions, RH rotating forward, LH rotating back.

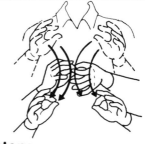

story
Open 9 shape both hands. Move down, link thumbs and index fingers, then pull apart, ending in 9 shapes. Repeat motion.

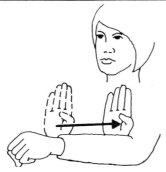

board
Run base of right B up left arm from wrist to elbow.

chalk
Mime writing on blackboard with chalk.

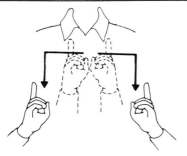

desk
D shape both hands, palms facing, thumbs almost touching. Draw apart and down.

bell
LH open B palm right, tips up. Strike right S against left palm and pull away. Repeat motion.

music
LH open B palm up, tips slightly right. Swing right M back and forth over left palm and forearm without touching.

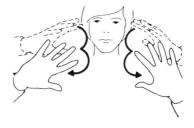

noise
Five shape both hands, index fingers held at ears. Shake hands outward.

attention
B shape both hands, palms placed on temples. Move forward parallel to one another.

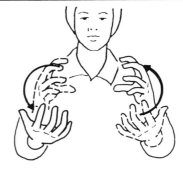

mess
Claw shape both hands, palms facing. Simultaneously twist LH inward and RH outward.

2 PRACTICE

Practice signing and saying the following phrases and short sentences. Fingerspell all words hyphenated letter by letter (e.g., m-o-t-h-e-r).

1. my toothbrush
2. t-h-e boy's towel
3. his daddy's bed
4. t-h-e baby's blanket
5. your bathtub
6. toilet paper
7. her laundry basket
8. t-h-e chalkboard
9. our gym class
10. t-h-e basement stairs
11. That i-s mommy's shampoo.
12. This i-s my doctor's bag.
13. their paper and pencils
14. grandfather's cigarettes
15. that mailman's letter
16. t-h-e room's windows
17. t-h-e vacuum cleaner's noise
18. this child's storybook
19. our television picture
20. this policeman's keys
21. your closet door
22. my bathroom floor
23. t-h-e kitchen cabinets
24. t-h-e girl's radio
25. these bedroom curtains

3.
SPECIAL VERBS
and
FUNCTION WORDS

SPECIAL VERBS

The verbs in this chapter are considered "special" because of their importance in everyday communication. They are used more frequently in general conversation than any other verb forms.

To be and *to have* are also special in that each form of these verbs has its own unique sign. They do not use the Signed English markers to indicate their form.

The verb *to do* uses markers for the forms *does* and *did*. However, the contractions *don't, doesn't,* and *didn't* all have special signs.

FUNCTION WORDS

Function words are those small words that give sentences their structure. They are not the key words in a sentence, but they are necessary in order for the meaning of the sentence to be clear. This sentence has no function words: He attends - game - week - friends. The meaning is not clear unless function words are added: He attends *the* game *each* week *with* friends.

Missing function words cause misunderstanding in communication situations. In Signed English the signs for function words are used as an important step for developing clear and satisfying English. Fingerspell the following function words:

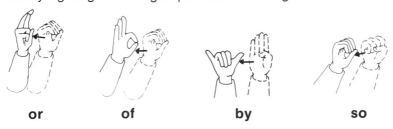

| or | of | by | so |

INFINITIVES

In Signed English an infinitive may be signed in either of two ways. Most people prefer to fingerspell the word *to* and sign the base verb.

t + **o** + **be** = **to be**

It is also acceptable to use the sign *to* with the base verb.

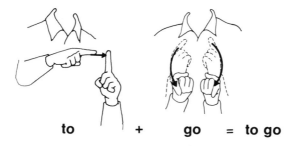

to + **go** = **to go**

SHOWING EMPHASIS

In Signed English, emphasis can be added to a sentence by using the signs for *need* and *must.* Many people also use the *must* sign for the phrase *have to.*

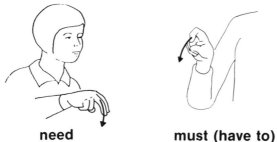

need   **must (have to)**

It is also acceptable to sign each word of the phrase *have to.*

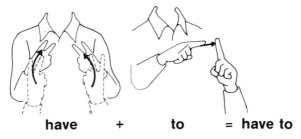

have + to = have to

CONTRACTIONS

Most contractions are formed by first making the base sign. Then form the appropriate manual letter from the chart below with your right hand and quickly twist it inward.

Contraction Parallels

English:	'd	'll	'm	n't	're	've	's
Manual Letter:	D	L	M	N	R	V	S

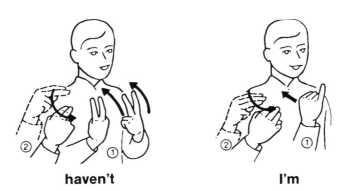

haven't   **I'm**

Five exceptions to the contractions' rule are *can't, won't, don't, doesn't,* and *didn't.* These words have their own unique signs which are illustrated in this chapter.

be
B shape RH palm left, tips up. Place index finger on mouth and move out.

am
Place right A on mouth and move out.

is
Place little finger of right I on lips and move out.

are
Place right R on lips, then move forward.

was
Place index finger of right W on lips and move back to right cheek.

were
Place right R on lips and move back to right cheek.

will
Place palm of right open B near right cheek and move out.

won't
A shape RH knuckles left. Jerk back over right shoulder.

would
Place palm of right open B near right cheek then move out. Repeat.

been
Place index finger of B shape RH on lips. Move out and form letter N.

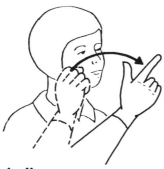

shall
S shape RH palm left. Place near right cheek and move out to L shape.

should
X shape RH knuckles down. Move down. Repeat.

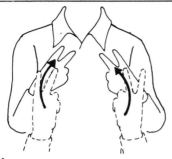

have
V shape both hands, palms in, tips up. Draw toward and touch chest.

has
S shape both hands, palms in. Draw toward and touch chest.

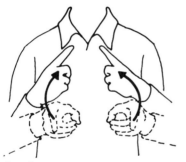

had
Place thumb and index tips of D shape hands on chest.

do
Claw shape both hands, palms down. Swing back and forth.

does
Claw shape both hands, palms down. Swing back and forth. Then add the 3rd person singular marker.

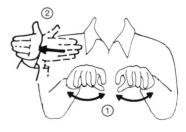

did
Claw shape both hands, palms down. Swing back and forth. Then add the irregular past verb marker.

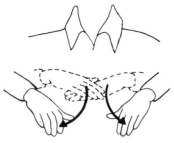

don't
Open B both hands, palms down, tips slanted toward one another. Place RH over LH and draw apart forcefully.

doesn't
LH open B palm down. Place right S over LH then draw hands apart forcefully.

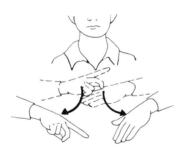

didn't
LH open B palm down. Place right D over LH then draw hands apart forcefully.

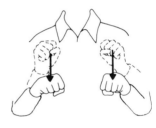

can (verb)
S shape both hands, knuckles down. Move down in forceful motion.

can't
One shape both hands, palms down, tips slanted toward one another. Strike tip of left index with tip of right passing on down.

could
S shape both hands, knuckles down. Move down in forceful motion. Repeat.

a
A shape RH. Move to right.

an
N shape RH palm in. Twist outward.

the
T shape RH palm in. Twist out.

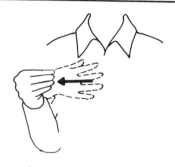

and
Five shape RH palm in, tips left. Move from left to right, closing into flat O.

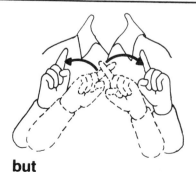

but
Cross index fingers and draw apart.

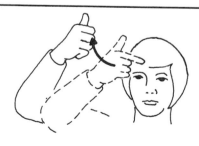

because
L shape RH palm in, index tip left. Place on forehead then draw back to right, ending in A shape thumb up.

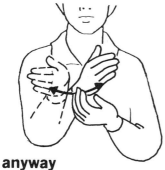

anyway
Curved LH open B palm up. Slap tips of fingers back and forth with little finger side of right open B.

matter
M shape both hands, palms in, tips facing. Alternately slap tips back and forth.

bit (small amount)
Hold RH palm up and flip thumb from under index finger several times.

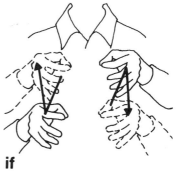

if
F shape both hands, palms facing, tips out. Move up and down alternately.

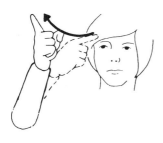

for
One shape RH palm in. Place tip on forehead, twist wrist, and point tip forward.

than
Bent open B shape both hands, palms down. Slap down left fingertips with right fingertips.

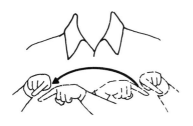

as

One shape both hands, palms down, tips out. Hold index fingers close together then arc from left to right.

like (adj./adv./prep.)

Y shape RH palm out. Move back and forth from left to right one or two times.

except

Grasp left index finger with right thumb and index finger and pull up.

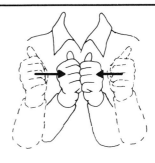

with

A shape both hands, knuckles facing, thumbs up. Bring together.

without

A shape both hands, thumbs up. Place together then draw apart, ending with fingers spread, both palms up.

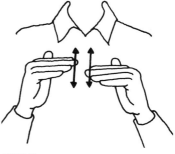

even

Bent open B shape both hands, palms down, tips almost touching. Alternately move up and down slightly.

either
L shape LH index tip out. Place base of right E on left thumb and arc to tip of index.

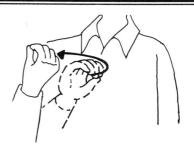

other
O shape RH tips out. Swing in semicircle to left, ending with tips up.

another
A shape RH knuckles down, thumb pointed left. Turn over so that knuckles face up.

any
A shape RH thumb up. Swing out to right.

each
One shape LH. Slide knuckles of right A, thumb extended, down back of left index finger.

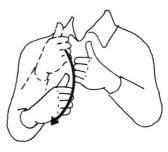

every
A shape both hands, thumbs up. Brush knuckles of right A down knuckles of left A.

question
Outline question mark in air with right index finger.

ask
Palms together tip out. Arc back to body, ending with tips up.

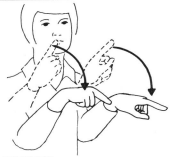

answer
One shape both hands, right index on mouth, left index a little in front of face. Move both forward ending with palms down.

who
Circle right index finger around mouth clockwise.

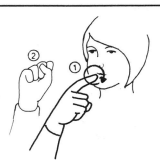

whose
Circle right index finger around mouth then form right S.

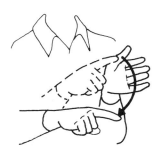

what
LH open B tips out, fingers slightly spread. Brush right index tip down across left fingers.

how
Hold backs of fingers together, palms down. Turn in and up.

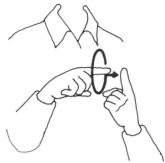

when
One shape LH palm in, held out from body. Circle LH with right index finger and then touch tips.

where
One shape RH. Wave from left to right.

why
RH open B palm in, tips up. Place tips on forehead and move out into Y shape.

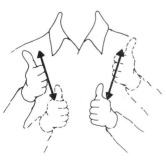

which
A shape both hands, palms facing, thumbs up. Move up and down alternately.

kind (of)
Place base of right K on left K. Then rotate right K around left K, ending in initial position.

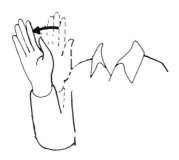

hi
Wave open palm from left to right.
(This word is often fingerspelled.)

bye-bye
RH open B palm down, tips out.
Wave up and down.

of course
Shake Y up and down.

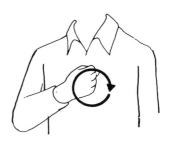

sorry
Circle right S on chest.

all gone
Place right C, palm in, on left
palm then draw out, closing into S
shape.

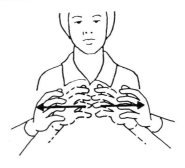

a lot (lots)
Claw shape both hands, palms
facing, fingertips touching. Move
hands apart quickly.

yes
S shape RH. Shake up and down at wrist.

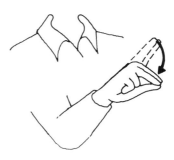

no
Snap middle finger, index, and thumb together quickly.

OK (okay)
Fingerspell O-K in quick succession as if one movement.

please
Rub right palm in clockwise circle against upper chest.

thank (you)
RH open B palm in, tips up. Place tips on chin or lips. Move out as if throwing a kiss.

you're welcome
W shape RH palm in. Place tips at mouth and arc forward and down, ending with palm up.

3 PRACTICE

Practice signing and saying the following sentences. Finger-spell all words hyphenated letter by letter (e.g., m-o-t-h-e-r).

1. She isn't a nurse.
2. I have a brother.
3. They don't have any soap.
4. What are you d-o-i-n-g?
5. What c-o-l-o-r is your room?
6. We have another television.
7. Do you have any string?
8. Please telephone your mommy.
9. I can't do my lesson.
10. He doesn't have a book.
11. Will they have a meeting?
12. What kind o-f oven does she have?
13. Who is that?
14. What's this?
15. Where were you?
16. Why did she do that?
17. Whose radio is this?
18. The children don't have any classes.
19. You can have either pencils o-r chalk.
20. Can you do this for me?
21. Each person has a toothbrush except D-a-n.
22. When will they have the toilet f-i-x-e-d?
23. These pictures are for your grandmother.
24. I haven't any shampoo.
25. Ask your mommy for a towel.

4.
THE BODY

POINTING TO BODY PARTS

To sign many parts of the body, just use the index finger to point to their locations on the body.

eye

muscle

Other body parts signed by pointing:

chin	finger	nose
elbow	fingernail	tongue
eyebrow	knee	tooth

SIGNING -ACHE WORDS

Sign words ending in -ache, (e.g., headache, stomachache) by making the sign for hurt in front of the painful part of the body.

hurt

One shape both hands, palms in, tips facing. Move back and forth toward one another.

headache   **stomachache**

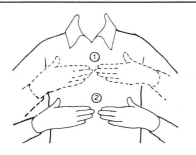

body
Open B shape both hands, palms in, tips facing. Pat chest, then stomach.

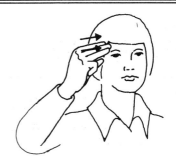

mind
Tap right temple with tips of right M.

brain
Place thumb of right C on forehead.

head
RH bent B palm down, tips left. Place tips on right temple then on chin.

hair
Grab hair with right thumb and index finger.

beard
Grasp chin with open B and draw down into flat O.

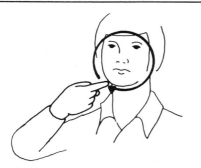

face
Circle face with index finger.

mouth
Outline mouth with right index finger.

voice
V shape RH palm in. Place tips on throat then arc upward and out.

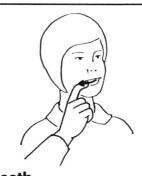

teeth
Outline teeth with bent right index finger.

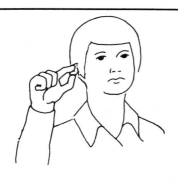

ear
Pinch lobe of right ear with right index and thumb (other fingers closed).

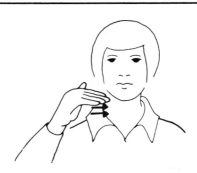

neck
Bent RH open B palm down, tips left. Tap right side of neck with tips.

arm
Clasp left wrist with right C and run C up to left elbow.

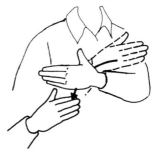

hand
Open B both hands, left palm slanted right, tips out. Draw little finger side of RH across left wrist in slicing motion.

stomach
Pat stomach with palm of right open B.

heart
Tap heart with right middle finger.

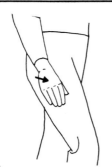

leg
Pat right thigh with right palm.

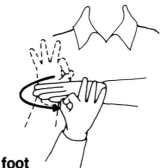

foot
LH open B palm down. Place thumb and index tips of right F on left thumb then circle around to left little finger.

sick
Five shape RH palm in. Tap forehead with middle finger.

sore
S shape both hands, palms down. Twist in opposite directions while moving toward each other. Repeat motion.

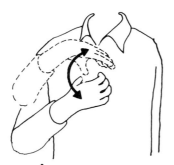

cough
C shape RH palm in. Place under throat with index and thumb touching chest. Rock up and down.

cold (noun)
Place right thumb and index on nose, then draw away as if using handkerchief.

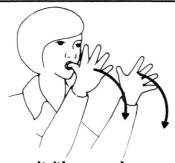

vomit (throw up)
Five shape both hands, palms facing, right thumb on mouth. Move both hands forward and down in sudden motion.

fever
RH open B palm out, tips left. Place back of hand on forehead.

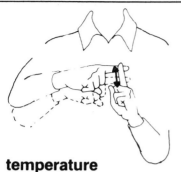

temperature
One shape both hands, left palm out, right palm down. Rub right index up and down back of left index.

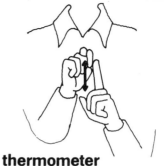

thermometer
One shape LH. T shape RH knuckles left. Rub right T up and down left index.

Band-Aid
S shape LH knuckles down. Draw right H over back of left S.

cut (noun)
S shape LH palm down. Draw right index to the right across back of left S.

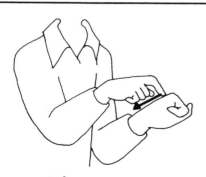

scratch
Scratch back of left S with right index finger.

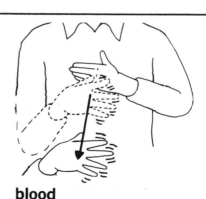

blood
LH open B palm in, tips right. Trickle right fingers down back of left (to indicate blood dripping).

medicine
Circle tip of right middle finger in upturned left palm.

pill
Mime popping pill in mouth with thumb and index finger.

operation
LH open B palm out. Draw tip of right thumb down left palm.

shot (hypodermic needle)
Place back of right V, thumb extended, on left upper arm. Push thumb against fingers, as if injecting needle.

menstruation (period)
Tap right cheek twice with flat fingers of right A.

pregnant
Intertwine fingers of both hands. Place in front of stomach then move out.

accident
S shape both hands, knuckles facing. Strike knuckles together.

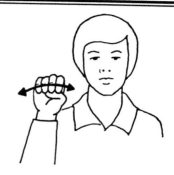

emergency
Shake right E back and forth from left to right.

trouble
B shape both hands, palms slanted out. Alternately circle inward toward front of face.

deaf
Point index finger to ear, then place index fingers of double B shapes together, palms down.

blind
Touch eyes with bent V.

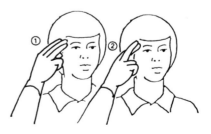

mentally retarded
Place tips of right M, then R, on right side of forehead.

clothes
Brush open palms down chest twice.

coat
A shape both hands. Trace shape of lapels with thumbs.

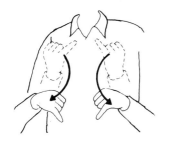

jacket
I shape both hands, palms in. Place fingers on chest and move down, outlining shape of lapels.

sweater
Claw shape both hands, palms in, tips in. Place on chest and move to waist, ending in A shapes.

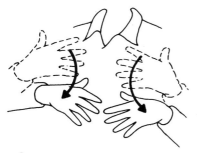

dress
Five shape both hands, palms in. Brush tips down chest while spreading hands apart slightly.

blouse
Bent B both hands, palms down, held at upper chest. Arc down, ending with palms up, little fingers against lower chest.

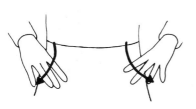

skirt
Five shape both hands, thumbs on waist. Brush down.

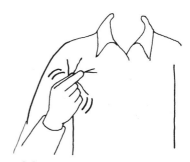

shirt
Grasp clothing on right upper chest with thumb and index finger of RH and tug slightly.

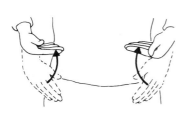

pants
Open B both hands. Place palms on hips and brush fingertips up toward waist.

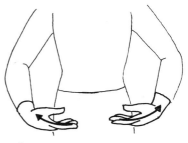

shorts
Open B both hands. Place fingertips on inside of thighs and move out, outlining bottom of shorts.

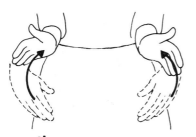

panties
Place tips of bent open B shapes on hip bones. Curve up slightly so that wrists rest on waist.

underwear
C shape LH palm in, tips on chest. RH open B palm in, tips down. Slide RH into left C.

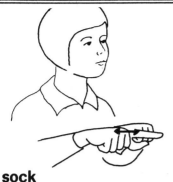

sock

S shape RH palm down. Brush back and forth along side of left index held tip out, palm down.

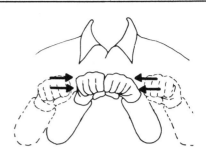

shoe

S shape both hands, palms down. Strike together several times.

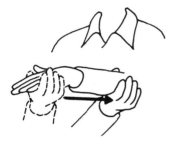

boot

B shape LH palm down, tips out. Place in right C which is held palm up, then slide right C up to left elbow.

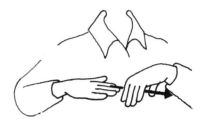

slipper

C shape LH palm down. RH open B palm down, tips left. Slide RH under left palm.

pajamas

Draw right fingers down over face ending in flat O. Form 5 shapes both hands, place on upper chest, then move down. (Sometimes fingerspelled P-J.)

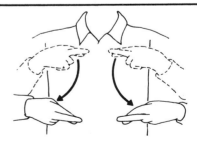

robe

R shape both hands, palms in, tips facing. Brush down chest.

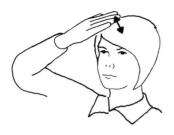

hat
Pat top of head with palm of RH.

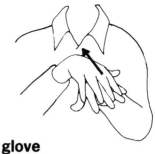

glove
Five shape both hands, palms down, tips out. Draw right fingers back over left fingers.

mitten
LH open B palm right, tips up. Outline with right fingers.

purse
A shape RH knuckles down. Hold as if carrying purse.

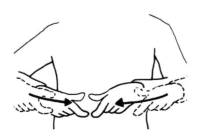

belt
Run index fingers and thumbs from each side of waist to middle of stomach (as if fastening buckle).

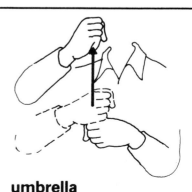

umbrella
Rest right S on left S and move RH up as if opening umbrella.

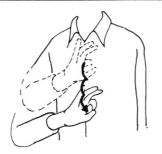

button
Curve index finger inside thumb.
Tap three times on chest beginning
at top.

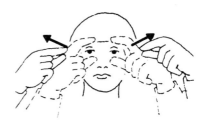

glasses
Place thumbs and index fingers at
sides of eyes then draw back, closing fingers (as if outlining frame of
glasses).

sunglasses
Circle eyes with index fingers and
thumbs.

hearing aid
Place right thumb, index, and middle finger on right ear (as if inserting aid).

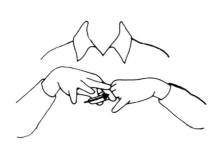

ring (jewelry)
Place right index and thumb
around left fourth finger and mime
putting on a ring.

watch (noun)
LH open B palm down, tips out.
Place tips of right W on left wrist.

⌁ PRACTICE

Practice signing and saying the following sentences. Finger-spell all words hyphenated letter by letter (e.g., m-o-t-h-e-r).

1. Grandmother has been sick.
2. The boy has a sore leg.
3. Did you scratch your sister?
4. Those people are deaf.
5. His aunt was i-n an accident
6. You have blood o-n your shirt.
7. Does she have a fever?
8. I can't f-i-n-d my robe.
9. The girl's mittens are o-n the table.
10. E-d-d-i-e had an emergency operation.
11. Does your daddy have a beard?
12. Mommy has a tissue for your nose.
13. How did you cut yourself?
14. Whose shoes and socks are those?
15. I'm okay. How are you?
16. That boy has to throw up.
17. The doctor's hypodermic needle is o-n his desk.
18. Where is your hearing aid?
19. Your umbrella is i-n the closet.
20. Do you have a stomachache?
21. The doctor has to t-a-k-e your temperature.
22. Thank you for your h-e-l-p.
23. Does your wife have a cold?
24. The boy's glasses are i-n the other room.
25. Each person has a watch except B-e-t-t-y.

5.
ACTIONS - 1

REGULAR PAST VERBS

Use the regular past verb marker to indicate the past tense of those verbs ending in *-ed*.

REGULAR PAST VERB MARKER

D shape RH, palm out.

walk   **+**   regular past verb marker   **=** **walked**

IRREGULAR PAST VERBS

Use the irregular past verb marker to indicate the past tense of those verbs not ending in *-ed*.

IRREGULAR PAST VERB MARKER

Open B shape RH, tips out. Slash to the right.

sit   **+**   irregular past verb marker   **=** **sat**

wake up
Hold index fingers and thumbs over eyes. Snap open into L shapes.

comb
Brush open fingers through hair twice.

brush (hair)
Brush knuckles of right A down hair twice.

brush (teeth)
Rub right index finger back and forth on teeth.

button up
F shape both hands, palms facing. Place tips together on chest and alternately twist back and forth.

tie
Mime tying a knot and pulling it tight.

zip
LH open B palm right, tips up.
Slide right X, palm in, up left
palm.

walk
Open B both hands, palms down,
tips out. Flap forward several times
alternately.

run
L shape both hands, index tips
out, LH a little ahead of right.
Hook right index finger around left
thumb. Wiggle L shape fingers
while moving both hands forward.

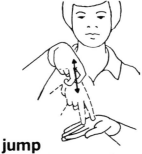

jump
LH open B palm up, tips out.
Place tips of right V in left palm
and pull up quickly, changing into
bent V shape. Repeat motion.

sit
H shape both hands, palms down,
left tips slanted right, right tips
slanted left. Rest right H on left.

stand
LH open B palm up. Stand tips of
right V on left palm.

kick

B shape both hands. Swing index finger side of RH up against little finger side of LH.

fall (verb)

LH open B palm up, tips out. Place tips of right V in left palm then flip forward and out, ending with palm up. (Sometimes made without LH as base.)

lie (recline)

LH open B palm up, tips out. Draw back of right V across left palm.

climb

RH bent V palm out. Move up in short circular movements.

hide

LH bent open B palm down. Place thumb of right A on lips then move down and under LH.

fight

S shape both hands, knuckles facing. Cross hands in front of body once or twice.

dance

LH open B palm up, tips out. Sweep right V over left palm several times.

ride

C shape LH palm right. Hook fingers of right H on left thumb and move both hands forward.

swim

Hands together palms down. Move forward and out (miming breaststroke).

sweep

Open B both hands, left palm up. Sweep little finger side of RH on left palm twice toward body.

rest

Open B both hands. Fold arms and rest palms on upper chest.

sleep

Draw open fingers of RH down over face, ending in flat O.

carry

Open 5 both hands, palms up, tips slanted left. Move from left to right or vice versa in front of body.

hold

S shape both hands. Place right on top of left as if grasping rope.

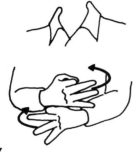

fix

F shape both hands. Place little finger side of right F on thumb side of left F. Twist hands in toward body.

drop

Hold right S at shoulder level. Drop into 5 shape, fingers and palm down.

open

B shape both hands, palms down, tips out, index fingers touching. Arc apart, ending with palms up.

close (verb)

B shape both hands, palms facing, tips out. Turn toward each other so that index fingers touch.

pick
G shape RH. Move up bringing index finger and thumb together.

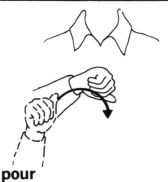

pour
A shape RH. Arc to left, as if pouring into cup.

draw
LH open B palm right, tips up. Draw right little finger down left palm in wavy motion.

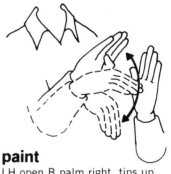

paint
LH open B palm right, tips up. Flap fingers of right open B up and down left palm.

cook
Open B both hands, left palm up, right palm down. Place right palm on left and flip over, as if flipping pancakes.

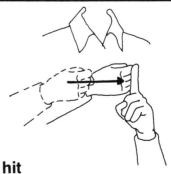

hit
Strike left index with right fist.

hug

S shape both hands. Cross arms on chest as if hugging something. (Sometimes H handshapes are used.)

touch

A shape LH palm down. Touch back of LH with tip of right middle finger.

throw

Hold right S over shoulder. Move forward into open handshape (as if throwing ball).

catch

LH open B palm right, tips up. Hit middle of left palm with index and thumb of right C.

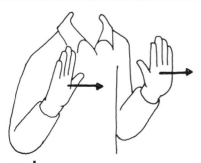

push

Open B both hands, palms out, tips up, left a little in front of right. Push out.

pull

A shape both hands, knuckles up, left ahead of right. Pull toward body in quick motion as if pulling a rope.

miss (verb)
One shape LH knuckles right.
Make sweeping pass by left index
with right claw shape ending in S.

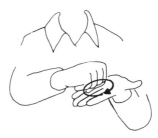

wash
Rub right S in circular motion on
upturned left palm.

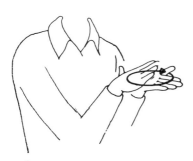

wipe
LH open B palm up. Rotate right
open B in left palm, as if wiping
something.

watch (verb)
Place back of right V just under
right eye. Move out over left hand
which is held palm down.

look
Point to eyes with tips of right V,
then twist and point out.

see
V shape RH palm in. Place tips at
eyes then move forward.

read
LH open B palm right, tips up.
Move tips of right V down left palm
in back and forth motion.

write
Mime writing in upturned left palm
with thumb and index finger of RH
(other fingers closed).

hear
Point index finger to ear.

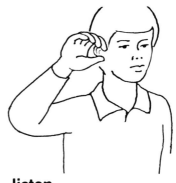

listen
Cup hand over ear.

smell
RH open B palm up, tips left. Hold
under nose and brush upward.

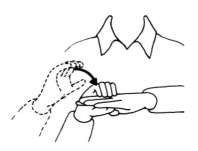

bite
B shape LH palm down, tips right.
"Bite" LH with fingers of right C.

blow

Place right O on right edge of lips. Bring out into open 5 toward left index finger which is pointed up.

smoke (cigarette)

Tap lips with tips of V shape RH palm in.

eat

Place tips of right flat O on lips. Repeat several times.

taste

Five shape RH palm in, tips up. Tap middle finger on chin once.

feed (verb)

O shape both hands, left in front of body, right on lips. Move right O down toward left O and shake both hands slightly.

teach

Flat O shape both hands. Hold at temples and move out twice.

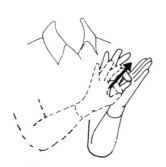

count

LH open B palm right, tips up.
Run thumb and index finger of
right 9 shape up left palm.

kiss

Place tips of right open B on
mouth and move back to cheek.

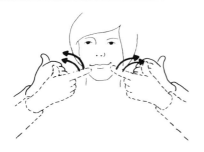

laugh

Place index fingers on sides of
mouth then quickly crook index
fingers two or three times.

cry

Place index tips under eyes and
draw down as if tracing tears.

smile

L shape both hands. Place index
fingers at sides of mouth and move
up to cheeks.

scream

C shape both hands, palms in.
Hold under chin then move up
and out.

say

One shape RH palm in, tip left. Hold at mouth and make small circle forward.

talk

Place index tips on mouth, alternately moving back and forth.

tell

One shape RH palm in. Place index tip on chin then move out, ending with palm up.

lie (falsehood)

Push right index finger across chin from right to left.

sing

LH open B palm up. Swing fingers of right open B above left forearm and palm in rhythmic motion.

sign (language)

One shape both hands, palms out. Alternately circle index fingers in toward body.

5 PRACTICE

Practice signing and saying the following sentences. Finger-spell all words hyphenated letter by letter (e.g., m-o-t-h-e-r)

1. Please don't fight with your brother.
2. Yes, I can swim.
3. He hugged and kissed his daddy.
4. Don't touch that lamp.
5. The mirror fell o-f-f the wall.
6. They washed and wiped the dishes.
7. Did you hit that boy?
8. My niece wrote a book.
9. Zip your pants and tie your shoes.
10. Who opened this door?
11. Eat everything o-n your plate.
12. The children threw their clothes o-n the floor.
13. They heard music o-n the radio.
14. When will we blow o-u-t the candles?
15. The man painted our room.
16. His friend is a dentist.
17. I fixed the kitchen sink.
18. Will you carry my books?
19. My grandfather saw the fight.
20. Watch me sign this story.
21. The woman sang a s-o-n-g.
22. Say thank you for the chalk.
23. She taught herself t-o sign.
24. The boy wiped o-f-f the table.
25. Who drew this picture?

ACTIONS ~2

THIRD PERSON SINGULAR VERB TENSE

Use the third person singular marker -s to form the present tense of most verbs.

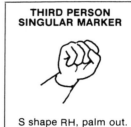

THIRD PERSON SINGULAR MARKER

S shape RH, palm out.

love + **third person singular marker** = **loves**

PARTICIPLES

Use the participle marker to form the participle of most verbs.

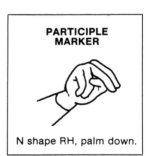

PARTICIPLE MARKER

N shape RH, palm down.

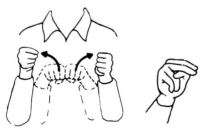

break + **participle marker** = **broken**

think
Place tip of index finger on forehead.

know
RH open B palm in, tips up. Pat forehead with tips.

understand
S shape RH palm in. Place on or near right temple then snap index finger up.

remember
Place thumb of right A on forehead, then drop down and touch thumb of A shape LH palm right.

forget
RH open B palm in. Draw tips across forehead from left to right, ending in A shape.

learn
LH open B palm up, fingers spread. Place fingertips of right 5 in left palm then move to forehead, changing into flat O.

dream

Place right index finger on forehead. Move up and out crooking finger several times.

hope

Touch forehead with right index finger. Raise open B hands so they face each other, RH near right forehead, LH at the left. Simultaneously bend (and unbend) fingers of both hands toward one another.

wish

W shape RH palm in. Place on chest and move down slightly.

promise

S shape LH palm down. Place right index finger on lips, move out into open B shape, and place against LH.

pretend

P shape RH palm out. Place index finger of right P on right side of forehead then circle forward.

want

Five shape both hands, palms up, fingers slightly curved. Draw back to body.

feel
Strike right middle finger upward on chest.

like (verb)
Place right middle finger and thumb on upper chest, then draw out and close fingers.

love
S shape both hands. Cross wrists and place over heart.

hate
Eight shape both hands, palms facing, tips out, left slightly in front of right. Flick middle fingers from thumbs.

worry
W shape both hands, palms slanted out. Alternately circle inward in front of face.

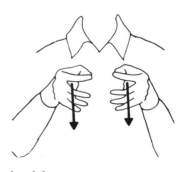

decide
F shape both hands, palms facing, tips out. Lower in decisive manner.

get

C shape both hands, right slightly above left. Move in toward body, closing into S shapes, right on top of left.

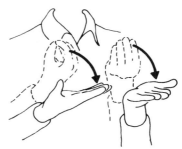

give

O shape both hands, palms up, left a little ahead of right. Move out, opening fingers.

bring

Open B both hands, palms up, one slightly behind the other. Move toward body as if carrying something.

take

Five shape RH palm down, fingers slightly curved. Draw up quickly, ending in fist.

come

One shape both hands, knuckles up, tips out. Bring tips up and back toward chest.

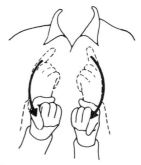

go

One shape both hands, palms and index tips in. Flip index tips out, ending with palms up.

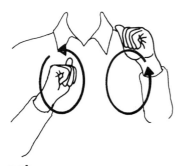

act
A shape both hands. Alternately move back in circles, brushing thumbs down chest.

behave
B shape both hands. Swing back and forth from left to right.

seem
RH bent B palm and tips left. Twist inward twice.

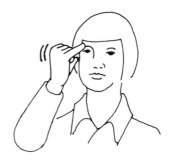

suppose
Tap right temple gently with right little finger.

let
L shape both hands, palms facing, index tips pointed slightly down. Bring to upright position.

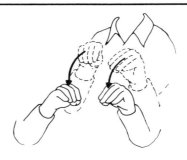

put
Flat O shape both hands, palms down. Move forward and down.

lead
LH open B palm in, tips right.
Grasp with fingers and thumb of
RH and pull to right.

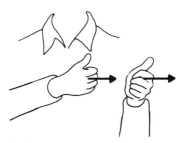

follow
A shape both hands, thumbs up,
right behind left. Move both forward simultaneously.

chase
A shape both hands, thumbs up,
right A behind left. Move right A
toward left in circular motion.

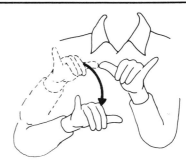

stay
Y shape both hands, palms down,
thumbs touching. Arc RH forward.

leave
Five shape both hands, palms
down, tips slanted left, left hand
in front of right. Draw back into A
shapes.

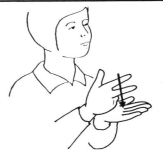

park (verb)
LH open B palm up, tips out.
Three shape RH palm left, tips
out. Drop base of right 3 in left
palm.

stop

LH open B palm up, tips out. Strike little finger side of right open B down on left palm.

start

Five shape LH palm and tips slanted right. Place right index between left index and middle fingers and make half turn.

finish

Five shape both hands, palms in. Turn suddenly so that palms and tips face out.

find

Five shape RH palm down, tips out. Close thumb and index finger and raise hand as if picking up something.

keep

V shape both hands, tips out. Place right V on left V. (Sometimes made with K handshapes.)

lose

Flat O shape both hands, backs of fingers touching. Drop into 5 shapes, palms down.

move
O shape both hands, palms down. Move from right to left or vice versa.

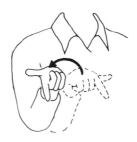

turn
L shape RH palm down. Turn so that palm faces up.

wait
Hold open hands palms up in front of body, left a little ahead of right. Wiggle fingers slightly.

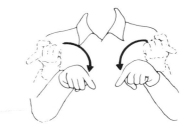

happen
One shape both hands, palms up, tips out. Twist toward each other, ending with palms down.

excuse
LH open B palm up, tips out. Brush edge of left palm twice with tips of RH.

bother
LH open B palm right, tips out. Strike little finger side of right B several times between thumb and index finger of LH.

change

A shape both hands, left knuckles up, right knuckles down. Place right wrist on left wrist, then reverse positions.

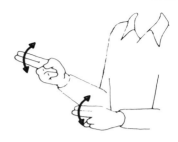

hurry

H shape both hands, palms facing, tips out. Shake up and down rapidly.

help

Place little finger side of left A, thumb up, in right palm. Raise right palm up.

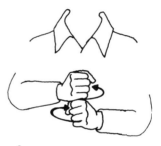

make

S shape both hands. Place little finger side of right S on thumb of left S. Twist hands in toward body.

work

S shape both hands, palms down. Hit back of left S with right S. Repeat motion.

play

Y shape both hands, palms in. Simultaneously twist back and forth.

live
L shape both hands, palms in, thumbs up. Place on chest and move up.

die
RH open B palm left, tips out. Turn so that palm faces up.

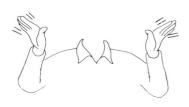

fly (verb)
Open B both hands held at shoulders. Flap from wrists two or three times.

crawl
LH open B palm up. Place back of right V on left forearm. Move down arm slowly while crooking and uncrooking fingers.

break
S shape both hands, knuckles down, thumbs and index fingers touching. Break apart.

cut (verb)
V shape RH palm in, tips left. Move fingers as if snipping with scissors.

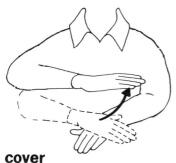

cover

Open B shape both hands, palms down, tips slanted toward one another. Slide right palm over back of left hand then lift up.

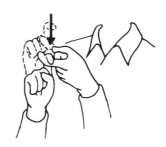

hang

X shape both hands. Hook right X over left X.

buy

Place back of right hand in left palm. Lift up and out.

shop (verb)

LH open B palm up, tips out. Place back of right flat O on left palm and move out twice.

visit

V shape both hands, palms in, tips up. Rotate away from body alternately.

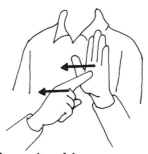

show (verb)

LH open B palm out, tips up. Place right index tip in middle of left palm and move both hands forward.

try
T shape both hands, palms facing. Move forward while arcing downward.

care
V shape both hands, palms facing, tips out. Strike index side of left V with little finger side of right V. Repeat.

mean (verb)
LH open B palm right, tips out. V shape RH palm down. Place tips of V on left palm then reverse, ending with right palm up.

use
A shape LH palm down. Circle right U clockwise over back of LH.

wear
A shape LH knuckles down. Circle right W over back of left A.

pay
LH open B palm up, tips out. Place middle finger of right P on left palm and flick out.

burn
One shape LH palm down, tip right. Flutter fingers of RH beneath left index.

shoot
L shape RH palm left, thumb up. Change to X shape, as if pulling trigger.

stuck
V shape RH palm in. Touch front of neck with tips of right V.

steal
Place right V palm down against left elbow. Pull back sharply toward wrist, ending in bent V.

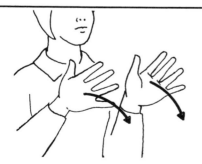

leave (alone)
Five shape both hands, palms facing, fingers spread, left hand slightly in front of right. Arc both hands forward and down.

tease
X shape both hands, left palm right, right palm left, little finger sides down. Slide right X forward on left X twice.

Practice signing and saying the following sentences. Finger-spell all words hyphenated letter by letter (e.g., m-o-t-h-e-r).

1. I forgot t-o tell you that.
2. She thinks she knows the answer.
3. Do you understand the question?
4. Tell me what you want.
5. My daddy hates liars.
6. He pretended t-o be my friend.
7. Your sweater was given to me.
8. They went to B-o-b-'s house.
9. I bought another blanket for the baby.
10. I don't know if Mommy wants t-o go.
11. It's okay if you don't want t-o eat that.
12. She goes to class every d-a-y.
13. Grandfather lost his keys.
14. The child burned her finger.
15. She helps make the beds.
16. Your hearing aid should be worn to school.
17. Hurry up and finish your work.
18. My brother likes t-o tease me.
19. Where did you find my boots?
20. Use your voice.
21. Show me the sore on your arm.
22. The child waited and waited for his turn.
23. The policeman's gun was stolen.
24. What happened to your hand?
25. I can't decide which blouse t-o wear.

7.
LEISURE TIME

PRESENT PROGRESSIVE VERBS

Add the *-ing* verb form marker to a base sign to form the present progressive form of a verb.

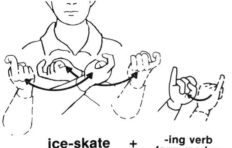

> **-ING VERB FORM MARKER**
>
> I shape RH, tips out. Slash to the right.

ice-skate   +   -ing verb form marker   = ice-skating

COMPOUNDS

Most compounds are formed by combining the two base signs that make up the compound. About 100 compounds are listed in the index of this book indicating where to find the base signs that form them.

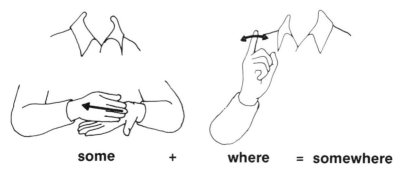

some   +   where   = somewhere

Some compounds have their own special signs. These compounds appear as separate entries in the text.

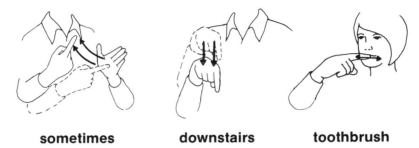

sometimes   **downstairs**   **toothbrush**

A few compounds are formed by two signs that differ in meaning from the English words.

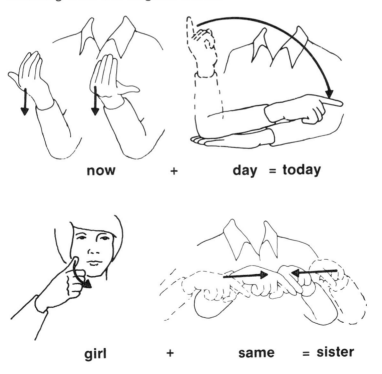

now   +   **day** = **today**

girl   +   **same**   = **sister**

Halloween

H shape both hands, palms in, tips up. Place tips under eyes and circle around to ears.

mask

M shape both hands, palms in, tips up. Place tips on bridge of nose then move to temples, ending with palms facing.

scare

S shape both hands, knuckles facing. Move toward one another sharply while opening into 5 shapes.

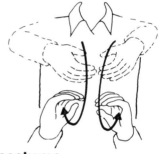

costume

C shape both hands, palms facing. Brush down chest.

ghost

Open 8 shape both hands, left palm up, right palm down. Close right thumb and middle finger around left thumb and middle finger. Then slip RH up in wavy motion and close both hands into 8 shapes.

witch

X shape both hands, left palm up. Place back of right X on nose, move out and down, and tap index tips.

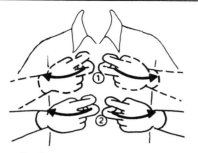

skeleton

Bent V both hands. Scratch outward across chest. Lower hands and repeat motion.

pumpkin

Thump back of left S, palm down, with middle finger of right P.

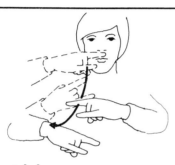

trick

Extend little and index fingers of both hands, palms down. Place right index under nose then pass under LH.

treat (noun)

T shape both hands. Turn forward and up.

jack-o'-lantern

C shape both hands, palms facing. Alternately move up and down sides of cheeks.

Thanksgiving

Open B both hands, palms in. Place tips on mouth, then arc out and down and up again.

Easter

E shape both hands. Circle away from each other.

parade

Four shape both hands, palms out, tips up, RH slightly back of LH. Move forward in little dips.

Hanukkah

H shape both hands, palms out, tips up. Place index fingers together and move away and up, outlining menorah.

Passover

Tap left elbow twice with thumb of P shape RH.

Christmas

Place elbow of right C on back of LH which is held before you tips right. Arc right C from left to right.

God

B shape RH palm left, tips slanted out. Arc up, back, and down, ending with tips up.

Jesus
Open B both hands, palms facing, tips out. Place tip of right middle finger on left palm then place tip of left middle finger on right palm.

pray
Place palms together, tips slanted up. Rotate toward body.

Santa Claus
C shape RH palm in. Place index finger on chin and arc down to chest.

reindeer
R shape both hands, thumbs extended. Place thumbs on temples and move up and out.

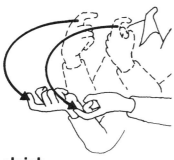

sleigh
X shape both hands, palms in, tips up. Arc outward ending with palms up and draw back to body.

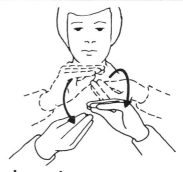

decorate
Flat O both hands, left palm up, right palm down. Touch tips and reverse positions several times.

present
P shape both hands. Bring up and turn out.

bow
Place knuckles of bent V shapes together, palms in. Draw apart into straight V shapes.

birthday
Four shape RH palm in, tips left. Place on upper left arm then flip over onto left forearm.

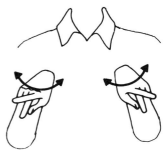

party
P shape both hands. Simultaneously swing hands to the left, then to the right, several times.

fun
H shape both hands, left palm down. Place right H on nose then on back of left H.

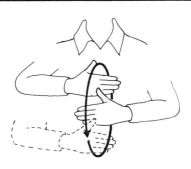

wrap
Open B both hands, palms in, left tips right, right tips left. Circle left hand with right.

card

LH open B palm up, tips out. C shape RH palm down. Slide RH off left palm.

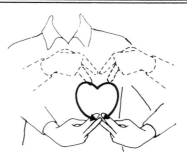

valentine

Outline heart shape on left chest with tips of V shape hands.

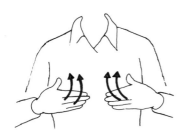

merry

Open B both hands, palms in, tips facing. Brush up chest twice.

surprise

Place index fingers and thumbs at edges of eyes. Snap open into L shapes.

secret

Tap thumb of right A against lips.

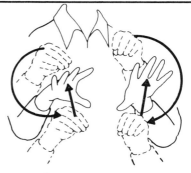

magic

Flat O shape both hands, tips out. Move away in semicircle, opening into 5 shapes palms out, tips up.

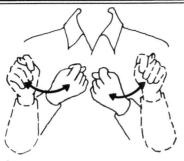

toy
T shape both hands. Swing in and out two or three times.

balloon
S shape both hands at mouth, left in front of right. Move apart, opening into cupped shapes (as if blowing up and holding balloon).

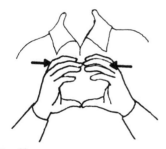

ball
Claw shape both hands, palms facing. Place tips together, outlining shape of ball.

doll
Brush down tip of nose twice with right X.

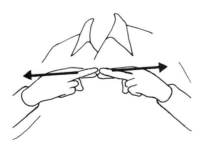

rope
R shape both hands, palms in, tips touching. Draw apart.

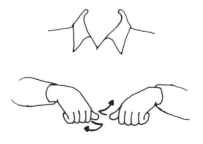

puzzle (noun)
A shape both hands, thumbs down. Make motion of fitting together.

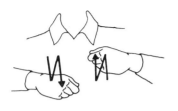

drum
Mime holding drumsticks and beating drum.

horn
C shape LH palm and tips right. S shape RH palm left. Hold RH at mouth and blow.

gun
L shape RH palm left, index finger out. Crook thumb down.

ice-skate
X shape both hands, palms up. Swing back and forth alternately.

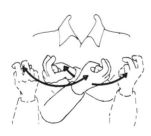

roller skate
Bent V shape both hands, palms up, right held near chest, left held out from body. Swing back and forth alternately.

sled
X shape both hands, palms up. Move slightly down and out (indicating runners).

slide
B shape RH palm down held at shoulder. Bring down in sweeping movement.

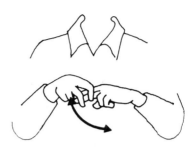

swing
Hook right V over left H, palms down. Swing both hands back and forth.

pail
S shape LH palm down. Place right index against left thumb, dip under, and place on left little finger.

shovel
LH open B palm up, tips out. Dig back of right open B into left palm and turn over toward body.

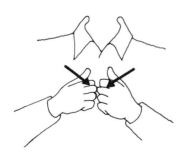

game
A shape both hands, palms in, thumbs up. Hit knuckles together once while moving hands down slightly.

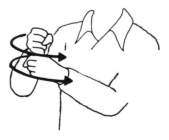

baseball
Mime grasping baseball bat with S shape hands and swinging at ball.

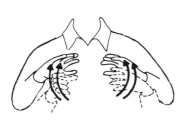

basketball
Mime holding ball then arc hands upward twice.

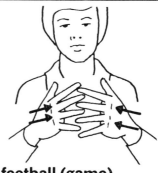

football (game)
Five shape both hands, palms in, tips facing. Mesh fingers together two or three times.

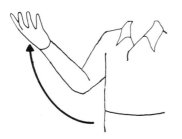

bowl (verb)
Mime throwing bowling ball.

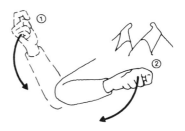

tennis
Mime swinging tennis racket.

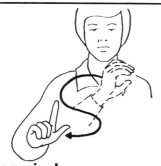

carnival
C shape RH palm left. Outline a "backward" S while changing to L shape.

roller coaster
R shape RH held up to left. Move down in a wavy motion, ending in C shape.

art
LH open B palm right, tips up. Draw right little finger straight down left palm. Repeat.

color
Five shape RH palm in. Flutter fingers at chin level.

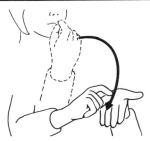

pencil
Place tips of right thumb and index finger on mouth then slide across upturned left palm.

pen
LH open B palm up, tips out. "Write" in palm with middle tip of right P.

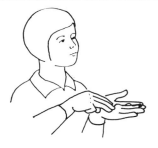

Magic Marker
LH open B palm up, tips out. Write across left palm with tips of M shape RH.

crayon
LH open B palm up, tips out. C shape RH. Move right thumb forward on left palm with small wave-like motion.

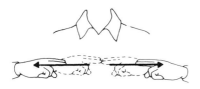

tape

H shape both hands, palms down, tips touching. Draw apart in straight line.

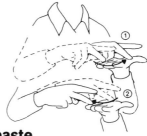

paste

LH open B palm up, tips out. Place middle finger of right P on left fingers, draw back over palm, turn over, and draw back to left fingertips.

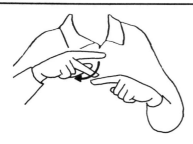

piece

One shape LH palm down. Strike middle fingertip of right P down against left index tip.

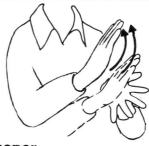

paper

Open B both hands, left palm up, tips out; right palm down, tips left. Brush base of right palm across base of left palm toward body twice.

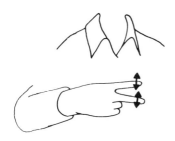

scissors

V shape RH palm in, tips left. Open and close fingers like scissor blades.

clay

Put hands together and move slightly as if molding clay.

black
Draw index finger across forehead from one brow to the other.

blue
B shape RH palm left. Shake back and forth slightly.

brown
Place index finger side of right B on cheek and slide down.

gray
Five shape both hands, palms in, tips facing. Move right fingers back and forth between left fingers. (Sometimes made like sign for *black,* using right G shape instead of index finger.)

green
G shape RH. Shake back and forth.

gold
Point right index finger to right ear then twist out, ending in Y shape.

orange
C shape RH palm and tips left. Place at mouth and "squeeze" into S shape. Repeat motion.

pink
Place middle fingertip of right P on lower lip and brush down to chin twice.

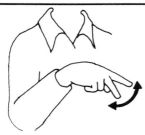

purple
Shake right P back and forth from wrist.

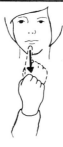

red
Brush lower lip with tip of right index finger. Repeat motion. (Sometimes made with R shape RH.)

white
Five shape RH palm in, tips left. Place tips on chest and bring out into flat O shape.

yellow
Y shape RH. Shake in and out.

Practice signing and saying the following sentences. Finger-spell all words hyphenated letter by letter (e.g., m-o-t-h-e-r).

1. Your black Halloween mask scares me.

2. Let's put the jack-o'-lantern o-n the table.

3. Please don't drop that big, orange pumpkin.

4. The witch rides o-n her broom.

5. Who has o-n the gray ghost costume?

6. Trick o-r treat!

7. Keep your black and white skeleton costume i-n its box.

8. The boy goes to his grandmother's house every Thanksgiving.

9. Red, white, and green are the colors o-f Christmas.

10. Christmas is Jesus' birthday.

11. Santa Claus' sleigh is pulled b-y eight reindeer.

12. Have you finished decorating your tree?

13. I'm dreaming o-f a white Christmas.

14. Can you hear the sleigh bells?

15. Grandfather brought you a present.

16. The Hanukkah candles are burning.

17. Look a-t this purple and yellow Easter hat!

18. My daddy is watching the football game o-n television.

19. Was your birthday party a surprise?

20. I got a valentine card f-r-o-m a secret friend.

21. She bought green wrapping paper and a gold bow.

22. What kind o-f doll did you get?

23. Let's say a thank you prayer to God.

24. The children need paper, scissors, crayons, and paste for their valentine cards.

25. Did you have fun a-t the roller skating party?

8. NATURE and ANIMALS

ICONIC NATURE OF SIGNS

Some signs seem to paint pictures of the things they represent. This iconic nature of signs is best seen in this chapter.

The sign for *elephant* outlines the animal's large, swaying trunk.

elephant

In the sign for *chicken*, you can see the bird pecking and scratching for food.

chicken

The sign for *hippopotamus* is based on the animal's enormous mouth and funny teeth.

hippopotamus

There is no mistaking the fact that your arm and hand represent the trunk and branches in the sign for *tree*.

tree

ADJECTIVES ENDING IN -Y

Add the adjective -*y* marker to change some nouns into adjectives.

ADJECTIVE -Y MARKER

Y shape RH, palm out.

dirt + adjective -y marker = **dirty**

ADVERBS ENDING IN -LY

Add the adverb -*ly* marker to change certain adjectives into adverbs.

ADVERB -LY MARKER

Y shape RH, palm out, index finger extended. Move down in wavy motion.

happy + adverb -ly marker = **happily**

outside

Cupped 5 shape LH palm right. Place fingers of RH against left palm and pull out, ending in flat O shape. Repeat motion.

yard (place)

LH open B palm down. Y shape RH palm down. Circle right Y over left hand and forearm.

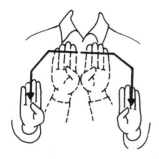

barn

B shape both hands, thumb knuckles touching. Draw apart and down outlining shape of barn.

tent

V shape both hands, palms facing, tips touching. Draw apart, ending with palms down.

bridge

Hold left open B in front of body palm down, tips right. Place tips of right V under left wrist then arc to elbow.

fence

Four shape both hands, palms in, tips facing. Place tips of middle fingers together then draw apart.

107

road
R shape both hands, palms down, tips out. Move forward.

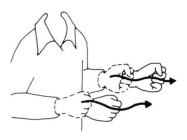

street
S shape both hands, palms facing, little finger sides down. Move forward.

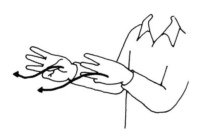

way
W shape both hands, palms facing, tips out. Move forward.

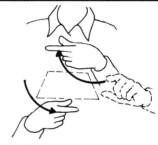

garden
G shape both hands, tips out. Move right G in front of left G, turning right tips left and left tips right (indicating square shape).

plant
Pass right P up, through, and over C shape LH palm right. (Sometimes *plant*, the verb, is signed by passing the tips of right P down through C shape LH.)

seed
Rub fingers of RH together while moving from right to left, as if dropping seeds into soil.

grow
Hold left C before body. Pass right flat O up through left C, spreading fingers as hand emerges.

tree
Five shape RH palm left. Place right elbow on back of LH and shake RH rapidly.

woods
W shape RH palm left. LH open B palm down, held across front of body. Place right elbow on back of LH then twist right wrist back and forth.

flower
RH flat O. Place tips on right side of nose then arc to left side.

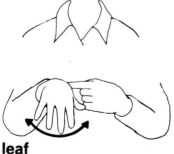

leaf
One shape LH palm in, tip right. Place right wrist over left index and move hand back and forth.

grass
B shape LH palm down, tips right. G shape RH. Outline left hand with right G.

hole
C shape LH palm and tips right, little finger side down. Circle with right index which is pointed down.

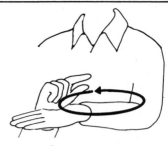

ground
LH open B palm down, tips right. Place base of right G on back of left wrist, then circle counterclockwise over elbow and return to original position.

dirt
Place back of RH, tips left, under chin. Wiggle fingers.

stone
S shape both hands, left palm down, right palm up. Tap back of left S twice with back of right S.

hill
RH open B palm down. Dip down and up, outlining shape of hill.

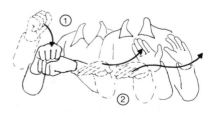

mountain
Tap back of left S with right S. Separate into open B shapes palms down, left higher than right. Move both hands up to left, outlining shape of mountains.

water
Tap lips (or chin) twice with index finger of right W.

beach
Open B both hands, palms down, left tips slanted right, right tips slanted left. Circle right B over left hand up to elbow and back.

ocean
O shape both hands. Open into 5 shapes and dip forward in wavy motion.

river
Place index finger of right W on mouth. Then move both hands forward, palms down, in rippling motion.

sky
Place RH open B, palm down, to left over head. Arc from left to right, ending with fingertips pointing to sky.

sun
Place right C against side of right eye.

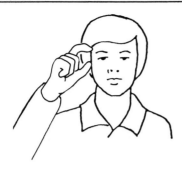

moon
Form little C with right thumb and index finger. Place at side of right eye.

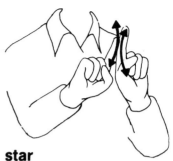

star
One shape both hands, palms out. Alternately strike index fingers upward against each other.

cloud
Cupped shape both hands, palms facing. Move from right to left with undulating motion. (Can also be made moving from left to right.)

weather
W shape both hands, left palm up, tips out; right palm down, tips left. Place right wrist on left then reverse.

thunder
S shape both hands. Draw left S back while moving right S forward. Repeat.

lightning
Hold right index finger up and zigzag down.

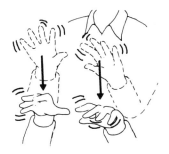

snow

Five shape both hands, palms down. Wiggle fingers while moving down slowly.

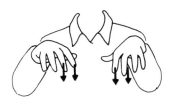

rain

Claw shape both hands, palms down. Move down sharply two or three times.

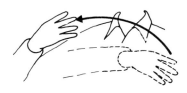

rainbow

Four shape RH palm in, tips down. Arc from left to right, outlining rainbow.

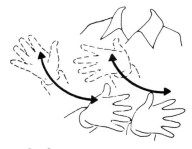

wind

Five shape both hands, palms facing, tips out. Swing back and forth.

smoke

Cupped 5 shape both hands, left palm up, tips slanted right. Place tips of RH in left palm then move up in spiraling motion.

fountain

Flat O shape both hands, palms facing, tips touching. Move out and apart while wiggling fingertips.

animal
Place tips of claw hands on upper chest and move back and forth toward one another.

cat
Place thumb and forefinger of right 9 at side of mouth and pull away twice (indicating whiskers).

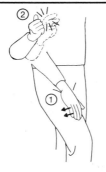

dog
Pat right thigh with RH twice then snap thumb and middle finger twice. (Can also be signed using either ① or ② alone.)

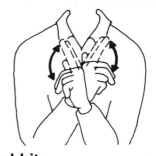

rabbit
H shape both hands. Cross at wrists then wiggle index and middle fingers up and down.

squirrel
Bent V shape both hands, palms facing, wrists touching. Tap tips of V shapes together at mouth.

raccoon
R shape both hands, palms in. Place tips under eyes and draw back to ears.

skunk
P shape RH palm down, index tip left. Place thumb on forehead and draw back over crown of head.

mouse
Strike tip of nose with right index finger.

rat
Brush down tip of nose with R shape RH palm left.

owl
O shape both hands. Place in front of eyes and twist inward slightly. Repeat motion.

bird
G shape right hand, tips left. Place on chin and snap index and thumb together twice.

butterfly
Hook thumbs palms in and flap fingers.

bug

Place thumb of right 3 on nose and crook index and middle fingers down.

bee

Place thumb and index finger of right F on right cheek. Move away into open B shape, then brush down cheek with right fingertips.

fly (noun)

S shape LH palm down. Curved RH open B palm left. Brush RH across back of LH, ending in S shape (as if catching a fly).

ant

Place base of right A on back of left claw hand which is held palm down. Move left claw forward in crawling motion.

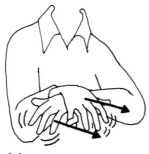

spider

Five shape both hands, palms down. Cross RH over LH, interlock little fingers, and wiggle all fingers while moving forward.

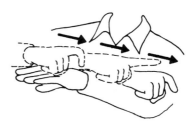

caterpillar

LH open B palm down, tips right. Rest knuckles of right X on back of LH. Crook and uncrook right index while moving hand up left arm.

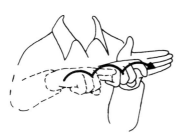

worm

LH open B palm slanted out.
Move right X across left palm
while crooking and uncrooking
right index finger (to indicate
wiggling worm).

snake

Place back of bent V under chin
then circle forward.

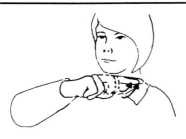

frog

Place right S under chin and flick
index and middle fingers out
twice.

fish

Open B both hands, left palm in,
tips right; right palm left, tips
out. Place left tips on right wrist.
Flutter right hand while moving
forward.

turtle

Place right A under curved LH.
Extend thumb and wiggle.

lizard

LH open B palm right, tips up.
Run right L up left palm in wiggly
motion.

farm

Five shape RH palm in, tips left.
Place thumb on left side of chin
and draw across to right side.

horse

H shape RH thumb extended.
Place thumb on right temple. Flap
H fingers downward twice.

pony

P shape RH. Place thumb knuckle
of right P on right temple. Twist
middle finger forward and down
twice.

cow

Place thumb of right Y on right
temple and twist forward.

sheep

Clip together tips of right V, palm
up, on left forearm (as if clipping
wool). Repeat motion.

goat

Flick tips of right bent V on chin
then on forehead.

pig
Place back of RH, fingers together, under chin. Flap tips down once.

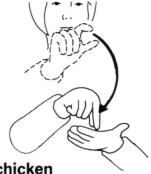

chicken
Place side of right G on mouth then place tips in left palm.

duck
Snap thumb and index and middle fingers together at mouth (to indicate duck quacking).

rooster
Three shape RH palm left. Tap forehead with thumb twice.

turkey
Place back of right Q on tip of nose then shake down in front of chest.

goose
LH open B palm down, tips right. G shape RH. Rest right elbow on back of left hand.

zoo
Five shape LH. Trace Z on left palm with right index finger.

cage
Hold right 5 in front of forehead palm in. Drop to chin.

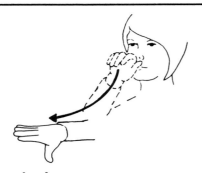

elephant
Place back of right curved open B on nose and trace trunk of elephant downward.

giraffe
Place right C on side of neck. Raise up, indicating long neck.

hippopotamus
Y shape both hands, left tips up, right tips down. Place right tips on left. Open wide and close again.

rhinoceros
C shape RH palm left. Place on nose and move out, ending in S shape.

lion
C shape RH palm and tips down, fingers slightly separated. Place on head and move back.

tiger
Claw shape both hands, palms in. Place tips on cheeks then move out. Repeat motion.

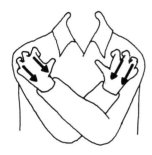

bear (noun)
Cross wrists of claw hands and scratch upper chest twice.

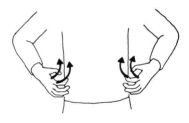

monkey
Claw shape both hands. Scratch sides of body with tips.

kangaroo
Curved open B both hands, tips out. Place right wrist on back of left wrist and hop forward twice.

alligator
Five shape both hands, left palm up, right palm down, all tips out. Place right palm on left, interlocking fingers, then lift RH up (indicating huge jaws).

seal
S shape LH palm down. Place right open B on top of left S and flap fingers down twice.

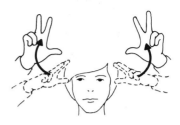

deer
Three shape both hands, palms out. Place thumbs on temples and move out and up.

wolf
Place tips of RH around nose then draw away into flat O shape.

fox
Enclose tip of nose with index and thumb of right F. Twist right wrist down and up.

camel
C shape RH palm left. Beginning at left, slide down toward right then up and down again, outlining hump.

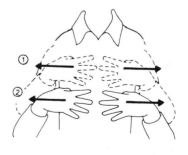

zebra
Four shape both hands, palms in, tips facing. Place over chest and draw apart. Lower hands and repeat.

Practice signing and saying the following sentences. Finger-spell all words hyphenated letter by letter (e.g., m-o-t-h-e-r).

1. Are you afraid o-f thunder o-r lightning?

2. She picked flowers for her mommy.

3. That brown bird is a barn owl.

4. The men dug a b-i-g hole i-n the ground.

5. Water makes the plants grow.

6. Can you count the stars i-n the sky?

7. We have a dog and a cat a-t h-o-m-e.

8. The boys are outside chasing butterflies.

9. I grew u-p o-n a farm.

10. Chickens are dirty animals.

11. My aunt is afraid o-f bees.

12. How many legs does a spider have?

13. The lion broke o-u-t o-f his cage.

14. Those two white rabbits are c-u-t-e.

15. The man was kicked b-y a horse.

16. A caterpillar is climbing u-p your back.

17. Is your dog brown o-r black?

18. T-h-e-r-e is a baby monkey i-n that cage.

19. Do you feel like playing outside?

20. The children rode two ponies a-t the farm.

21. The cow was hit b-y lightning.

22. Time to put the turkey i-n the oven.

23. Has anyone seen my p-e-t mouse?

24. The ocean water is c-o-l-d.

25. You shouldn't feed the zoo animals.

9. DESCRIPTIONS

COMPARING TWO PEOPLE OR THINGS

To sign the comparative form of an adjective, add the comparative -er marker to the base sign.

COMPARATIVE -ER MARKER
A shape RH, palm left, thumb up. Jerk upward.

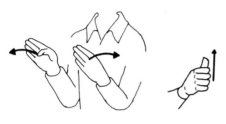

big + **comparative -er marker** = **bigger**

COMPARING THREE OR MORE PEOPLE OR THINGS

To sign the superlative form of an adjective, add the superlative -est marker to the base sign.

SUPERLATIVE -EST MARKER
A shape both hands, thumbs up. Brush knuckles of right A up knuckles of left A.

big + **superlative -est marker** = **biggest**

USING MORE AND MOST

If the comparative and superlative forms are preceded by the words *more* or *most,* then sign these words separately from the base sign.

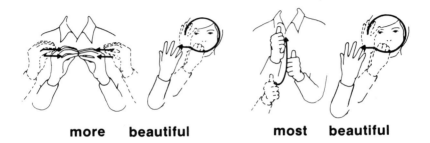

| more | beautiful | most | beautiful |

Note: The sign for the superlative *-est* marker and the word *most* are the same. Whether you sign it before or after the base sign determines its meaning.

USING UN- TO SHOW OPPOSITE OF

The opposite of marker is signed before the base sign to form the prefix *un-.*

OPPOSITE OF
MARKER

Place thumb of A shape RH under chin and brush forward.

| opposite of marker | + | **happy** | = **unhappy** |

good

Open B both hands, palms in, tips slanted up. Place right tips on mouth then move out and down, placing back of hand in left palm.

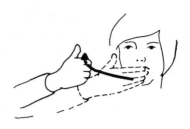

better

RH open B palm in, tips left. Place tips on chin then move upward into A shape with thumb extended.

best

RH open B palm in. Place at mouth and move out. Then form A shapes, thumbs up. Brush right A up against left A.

bad

Place tips of right open B on mouth then twist out and down.

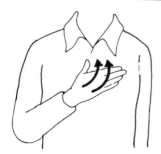

happy

RH open B palm in, tips left. Brush up chest twice with quick, short motion.

funny

Brush tip of nose twice with tips of right N.

sad

Five shape both hands, palms in, fingers slightly curved, LH a little below RH. Hold in front of face and drop slowly.

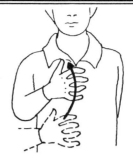

angry

Claw shape RH tips on chest. Draw up and out in forceful manner.

fine

Five shape RH palm left. Place thumb on chest and move slightly up and out.

grumpy

Hold right claw shape in front of face and crook fingers several times.

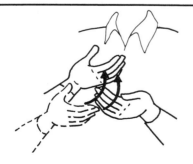

easy

Cupped LH open B palm up. Brush up back of left fingers twice with tips of right open B.

difficult

Bent V shape both hands, palms in, knuckles facing. Strike the knuckles together in up and down movements.

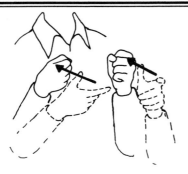

fast
L shape both hands, palms facing, index tips out. Draw back quickly into S shapes.

slow
Draw palm of RH slowly up back of LH.

loud
Place right index at right ear, then shake S shape both hands in front of body.

quiet
Open B shape both hands. Cross at mouth with right index finger on lips. Draw apart ending with palms down.

right (correct)
One shape both hands, tips out. Strike base of left index with little finger side of RH.

wrong
Strike chin with knuckles of Y shape RH.

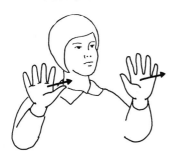

wonderful
Five shape both hands, palms out.
Push up and out.

terrible
Eight shape both hands. Place
on temples. Snap forward into 5
shapes, palms out.

dangerous
A shape both hands, thumbs up.
Bring right A up and place wrist on
back of left wrist.

afraid
Open 5 both hands, palms in, tips
facing. Move back and forth several times, as if shaking in fright.

alone
One shape RH palm in, tip up.
Circle counterclockwise.

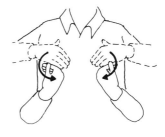

tired
Bent open B shape both hands,
palms in. Place tips on chest then
let hands drop, ending with little
finger sides against chest.

hungry
Draw tips of claw hand down upper chest.

thirsty
Point right index finger to throat and draw down.

lazy
L shape RH palm in. Tap chest twice just below left shoulder.

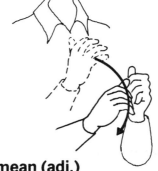

mean (adj.)
A shape LH thumb up. Claw shape RH thumb extended. Brush right knuckles down left knuckles.

nice
B shape LH palm and tips slanted right. Slide right N forward on left index finger.

friendly
Five shape both hands, palms in. Hold near corners of mouth and wiggle fingers while moving slightly outward and upward.

careful
V shape both hands, tips out.
Place right V on left then circle
both hands forward and back.

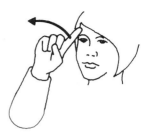

smart
Place right index on right temple
then move out quickly.

silly
Y shape RH. Shake in front of
nose.

strange
C shape RH. Place at right side of
face and arc across eyes to lower
left side of face.

proud
A shape RH palm out, thumb
down. Place on lower chest and
draw up slowly.

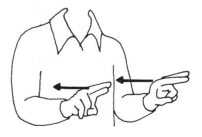

ready
R shape both hands, palms down,
tips out. Move from left to right.

cute
Place index and middle fingers on chin. Move down, closing over thumb.

pretty
Five shape RH palm in, tips up. Circle face from right to left ending in flat O.

beautiful
Five shape RH palm in, tips up. Circle face from right to left ending in flat O. Then spread fingers, palm in, tips up.

ugly
X shape RH palm down. Draw across nose from left to right.

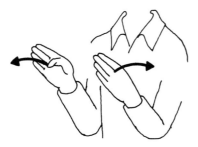

big
B shape both hands, palms facing, tips out. Move away from one another.

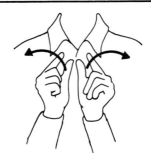

great
G shape both hands, palms and tips out. Arc hands apart.

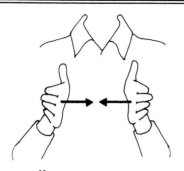

small
Open B both hands, palms facing, tips out. Draw close together.

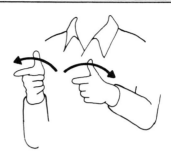

large
L shape both hands, palms facing, thumbs up. Arc hands apart.

hot
Place tips of right claw on mouth. Twist wrist quickly so that palm faces down.

warm
Place tips of right O at mouth then open up fingers into 5 shape.

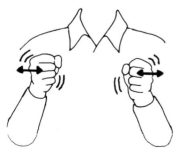

cold (adj.)
S shape both hands. Draw hands close to body and "shiver."

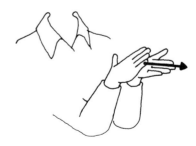

clean
Open B both hands, left palm up, tips out; right palm down, tips left. Brush right palm across left as if wiping clean.

new

LH open B palm up, tips out. Brush back of right open B inward across left palm in a scooping motion.

old

Place right S under chin then move down in wavy motion.

wet

Five shape both hands, palms in, fingers slightly curved. Place right index tip on mouth then drop both hands into flat O shapes.

dry

Draw bent index finger from left to right across chin.

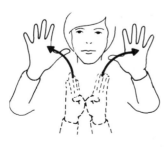

bright

B shape both hands, palms facing, tips up. Spread fingers and turn palms out.

dark

Open B both hands, palms in, tips up. Cross in front of eyes.

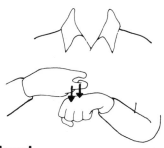

hard
S shape LH palm down. Hit back of left S with middle finger of right bent V. Repeat motion.

soft
Claw shape both hands, palms up. Lower into flat O shapes palms up. Repeat.

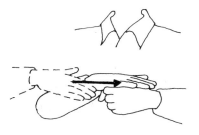

full
S shape LH knuckles right. Brush right palm across left S toward body.

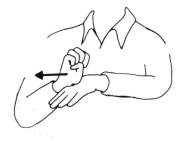

empty
LH open B palm down, tips out. Move base of right E out across back of LH.

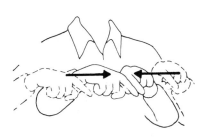

same
One shape both hands, palms down, tips out. Bring index fingers together.

different
Cross index fingers and pull apart so that fingers point outward. Repeat.

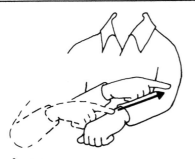

long
A shape LH knuckles down, arm extended. Run right index finger up left arm.

tall
LH open B palm out, tips up. Run right index finger up left palm.

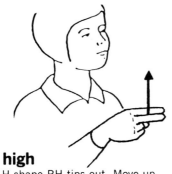

high
H shape RH tips out. Move up several inches.

low
L shape RH palm down. Move down.

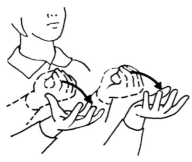

many
O shape both hands, tips up. Snap open quickly into 5 shapes palms up.

few
Loose A shape RH palm up. Pass thumb along first two fingers while opening them up.

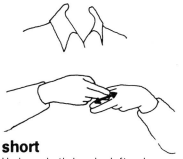

short

H shape both hands, left palm right, tips out; right palm in, tips left. Rub right H back and forth on top of left H.

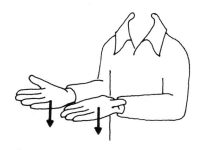

heavy

Open B both hands, palms up, tips out. Lower slowly.

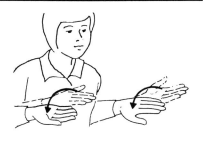

dead

Open B both hands, right palm down, left palm up. Simultaneously turn hands over to the right, reversing palm positions.

strong

Hold left forearm up. Outline shape of left bicep with the cupped RH.

sharp

LH open B palm and tips down. Place right middle finger on back of LH and jerk up and out.

fat

Hold claw hands on cheeks, then move away (indicating puffy, fat face).

sweet
RH open B palm in, tips up. Place tips on chin and brush down.

sour
Place right index finger on chin, palm left. Twist so that palm faces in.

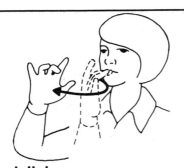

delicious
Place tip of right middle finger on lips and twist out.

important
F shape both hands, palms facing, tips out. Draw up in semicircle until index fingers and thumbs touch.

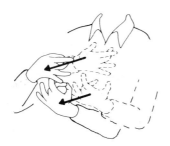

interesting
Place open tips of middle fingers and thumbs on chest, RH above LH. Move out, closing into 8 shapes.

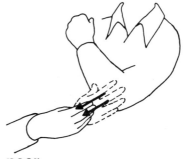

poor
Stroke left elbow with right fingers twice.

favorite
Five shape RH palm in. Tap middle finger on chin twice.

true
Place right index on mouth then move straight out. Repeat.

real
One shape RH palm left. Place finger on lips and move up and out.

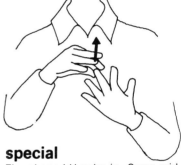

special
Five shape LH palm in. Grasp middle finger with right thumb and index and pull up.

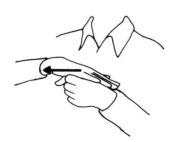

enough
S shape LH knuckles right. Brush right palm over left S away from body.

well (adj. & adv.)
LH open B palm up. W shape RH palm in. Place tips on mouth, then move out and down to left palm.

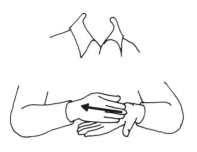

some

LH open B palm up. Draw little finger side of right open B across left palm.

both

V shape RH palm in. Place in left C which is held palm in, then draw down and out.

all

Open B both hands, left palm up, right palm down. Circle left with right, ending with back of RH resting in left palm.

nothing

S shape RH. Place knuckles under chin and flick out into 5 shape palm out.

more

Flat O shape both hands, palms and tips facing. Tap tips together twice.

most

A shape both hands, thumbs up, left A slightly higher than right. Brush knuckles of right A up knuckles of left A.

Practice signing and saying the following sentences. Finger-spell all words hyphenated letter by letter(e.g., m-o-t-h-e-r).

1. Be careful around those dangerous animals!
2. Don't be s-o grumpy!
3. He was the funniest person a-t the party.
4. I'm sorry I was s-o silly.
5. The basket is full o-f wet laundry.
6. He's tired o-f living alone.
7. The rhinoceros is the ugliest animal i-n the zoo.
8. M-a-r-y-'s favorite story is "The Three Little Pigs."
9. Do you want some more crayons?
10. She's really smarter than her older brother.
11. I'm not thirsty but I am hungry.
12. That is the most beautiful cat I've e-v-e-r seen.
13. Are you ready t-o light the fire?
14. The little boy walked quietly i-n-t-o the dark room.
15. What she said was untrue.
16. The mailman was bitten b-y the unfriendly dog.
17. My wife thinks her work is unimportant.
18. The sky looks cloudy.
19. Grandmother cooked a delicious turkey l-a-s-t Thanksgiving.
20. Which do you like better, ice skating o-r roller skating?
21. Rainy weather makes me feel unhappy.
22. Could you please turn the television louder?
23. Is your m-o-t-h-e-r shorter than your sister?
24. This will be your most difficult j-o-b.
25. A policeman's work must be v-e-r-y interesting.

FOOD

SOME UNUSUAL COMPOUNDS
FOR FOODS

Foods that are signed by combining the base signs of the two English words that make up the compound word (e.g., *black + berry = blackberry, water + melon = watermelon,* etc.) are listed in the index.

Here are some compounds for foods that are different.

lemon	+	drink		lemonade
K	+	drink	=	Kool-Aid

red + berry = raspberry   P + nut = peanut

food
Place tips of flat O on mouth.

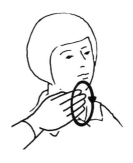

breakfast
B shape RH palm in, tips left.
Rotate tips at mouth.

lunch
Index tip of right L, palm in,
rotates in small circle in front
of mouth.

dinner
D shape RH palm in. Rotate at
mouth.

picnic
Place right palm on left palm. Lift
both hands up until tips touch
mouth.

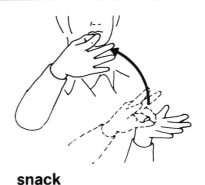

snack
LH open B palm up, tips out. Place
thumb and index tips of right F in
left palm, then raise to mouth.

dish

Place tips of curved open B shapes together. Arc back so that wrists touch, outlining dish.

plate

Five shape both hands, palms in, middle fingers touching. Circle back toward body ending with thumbs touching.

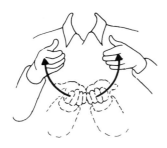

bowl (noun)

Hold cupped hands together palms up. Move apart and up, outlining shape of bowl.

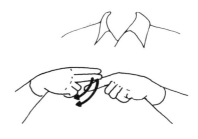

knife

Strike tips of right U against left index and move out sharply. Repeat motion.

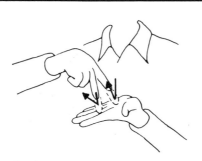

fork

LH open B palm up, tips right. Tap left palm with tips of right V.

spoon

LH open B palm up. Place back of right H on left palm then raise to mouth, as if eating from spoon. Repeat motion.

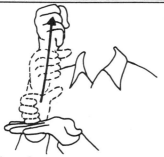

bottle
Place right C in left palm. Lift up closing into S shape.

glass (drinking)
LH open B palm up. Place little finger side of right C on left palm, then raise up, indicating shape of tall glass.

cup
LH open B palm up. Place little finger side of right X in left palm.

napkin
Place tips of right fingers on mouth and make small circle clockwise.

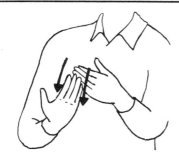

bread
LH open B palm in, tips right. Draw little finger side of right hand down back of left fingers several times.

cracker
Tap left elbow several times with right A.

butter
LH open B palm up, tips out.
Brush twice with tips of right H.

catsup (ketchup)
K shape RH palm out. Shake to
left side.

mayonnaise
LH open B palm up, tips out.
Place tips of right M on heel of
left palm and brush inward.

mustard
LH open B palm up, tips out.
Circle tips of right M in left palm.

jelly
Dip right J shape into upturned
palm of LH.

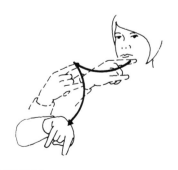

syrup
Extend right little and index fingers. Wipe chin with index and flip
wrist out.

sugar
H shape RH palm in. Stroke tips down chin twice.

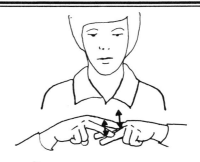

salt
Tap right V on back of left V two or three times. (Sometimes the fingers of the right V move alternately against fingers of left V.)

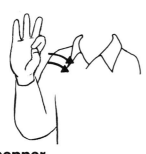

pepper
F shape RH. Mime shaking pepper shaker down to left.

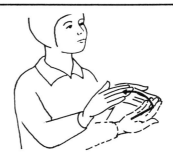

pancake
LH open B palm up, tips out. Slide back of RH up left palm then flip RH over (as if flipping a pancake).

cereal
LH open B palm up, tips right. Place back of right C in left palm then lift to mouth.

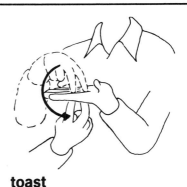

toast
Place tips of right V in left palm. Circle under and touch back of LH.

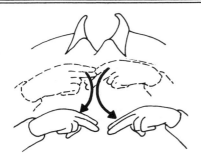

egg
H shape both hands, palms in. Hit left H with right H then draw hands apart.

bacon
H shape both hands, palms down, tips touching. Draw away in wavy motion.

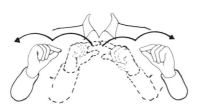

sausage
G shape both hands, palms and tips out, index fingers touching. Draw apart while opening and closing fingers, outlining links.

sandwich
Open B both hands, palms up. Slide right hand between thumb and fingers of LH (as if inserting filling into sandwich).

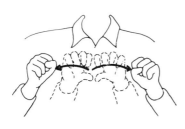

hot dog
Claw shape both hands, palms down, index fingers almost touching. Draw apart and close into S shapes.

hamburger
Clasp hands together, reverse position, and clasp together again, as if forming patty.

french fries
F shape RH palm down. Bounce to right.

cheese
Twist heel of right palm on heel of left palm.

meat
LH open B palm in, tips right. Wiggle flesh between left thumb and index with right thumb and index.

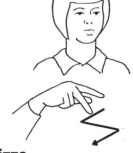

pizza
P shape RH, palm down. Draw Z shape in air with middle fingertip of right P.

salad
Three shape both hands, palms up, fingers curved. Mime tossing salad with small upward movements.

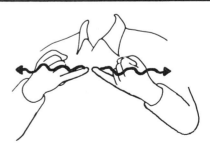

spaghetti
I shape both hands, palms in, tips touching. Wiggle away from each other.

noodle
N shape both hands, palms down, index fingers touching. Wiggle away from each other.

rice
LH open B palm up, tips slanted right. Place back of right R in left palm then move up to mouth. Repeat motion.

sauce
LH open B palm up. Circle right A, thumb down, over left palm, as if pouring.

soup
Place back of RH in left palm, then move up to mouth as if drinking soup. Repeat motion.

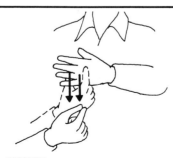

gravy
LH open B palm in, tips right. G shape RH. Grasp bottom of left palm with right index and thumb then slip fingers off into closed G. Repeat.

salad dressing
Mime pouring dressing on salad with A shape RH thumb down.

fruit
Place the thumb and index of right F on right cheek. Twist, ending with palm in.

apple
Press knuckle of right index finger into right cheek and twist forward.

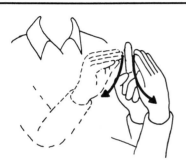

banana
Hold left index finger up. Go through motions of peeling a banana with tips of right flat O.

berry
Twist cupped RH around left little finger.

cherry
V shape LH palm down, tips right. Twist left index then middle finger with tips of right flat O.

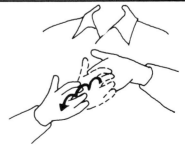

grape
LH open B palm in, tips down. Hop curved right fingers down back of LH, indicating a bunch of grapes.

lemon
L shape RH palm left, thumb in.
Tap chin with thumb.

orange
C shape RH palm and tips left.
Place at mouth and "squeeze"
into S shape. Repeat motion.

melon
S shape LH palm down. Flick right
middle finger against back of left S
(as if thumping melon).

strawberry
Nine shape RH. Place index and
thumb on mouth and flick out.

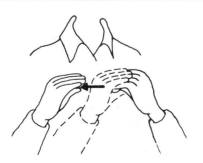

pear
LH flat O palm and tips right.
Stroke left tips with right fingers,
ending in flat O shape RH.

peach
Place tips of RH on right cheek,
thumb under chin. Stroke down to
right, ending in flat O.

pineapple
Twist middle finger of right P on right cheek.

vegetable
V shape RH. Touch right side of cheek with index finger then twist inward, ending with middle finger on cheek.

bean
One shape LH palm right, tip out. Strike twice with tips of right G.

carrot
Hold right S up to mouth and twist slightly, as if eating carrot.

corn
Hands face each other in front of mouth as if holding an ear of corn. Rotate slightly.

pea
One shape LH palm in, tip right. Tap from base to tip with right X.

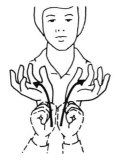

spinach
S shape both hands, palms facing, thumbs touching. Spread apart into claw shape hands, palms up.

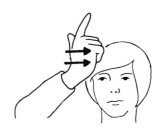

lettuce
Tap base of right L against right temple twice.

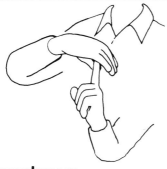

mushroom
C shape RH palm down, fingers left. Support with left index tip.

tomato
LH flat O palm and tips down. Brush right index down lips then down side of left flat O.

potato
S shape LH palm down. Tap back of LH with fingertips of right bent V.

onion
Twist X at corner of eye.

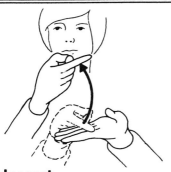

dessert
Place little finger side of right D on left palm, then raise to lips.

nut
Flip thumb out from under top teeth.

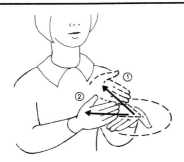

pie
Mime cutting slice of pie using left palm as pie and edge of right little finger as knife.

popcorn
S shape both hands, palms in, knuckles up. Snap index fingers up alternately.

raisin
LH open B palm in, tips down. Hop tip of right R down back of left B.

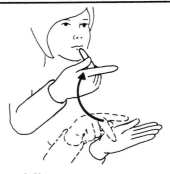

pudding
LH open B palm up, tips out. Place middle finger of right P in left palm then move up to mouth.

chocolate

Place thumb of right C on back of left hand and circle counterclockwise.

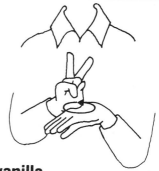

vanilla

LH open B palm down. Circle base of right V counterclockwise on back of LH.

lollipop

L shape RH palm left. Place index tip on mouth and brush down lips twice.

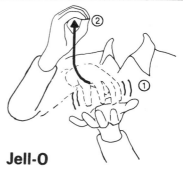

Jell-O

LH open B palm up, tips slightly right. C shape RH palm down. Wiggle right fingers over left palm and draw up into O shape.

ice cream

Hold right S at mouth then move down twice. (Mime licking an ice cream cone.)

gum (chewing)

Place tips of right V on right cheek and bend up and down rapidly.

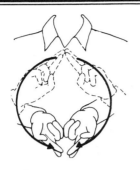

doughnut
R shape both hands, palms out, fingers touching. Turn over, ending with R shapes touching, palms up.

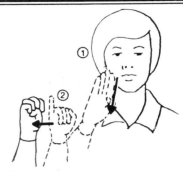

brownie
Place the right B against the right cheek. Slide down and quickly fingerspell I-E.

cookie
LH open B palm up, tips out. Place tips of RH in left palm and twist as if cutting out cookies.

cake
LH open B palm up, tips out. Hold right claw, tips down, over left palm then lift up while spreading fingers.

candy
Place right index finger just below right side of mouth and twist.

Popsicle
V shape RH palm in. Draw down over mouth and chin. Repeat.

drink
Mime holding and drinking glass of water with C shape RH.

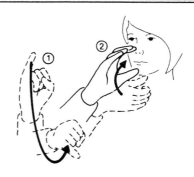

juice
Form letter J then raise cupped hand to mouth as if drinking.

milk
Claw shape both hands, palms facing. Alternately squeeze down into S shapes, as if milking cow.

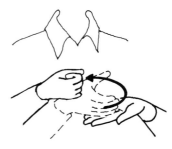

cream
LH open B.palm up, tips out. Pass right C over left palm, closing into S shape (as if skimming cream).

coffee
Place right S on left S and make a grinding motion counterclockwise.

tea
Place thumb and index tips of right F in left O and stir.

wine
W shape RH palm left. Circle at right cheek.

beer
Place right B against right cheek and circle forward.

pop
O shape LH palm and tips right. Put right thumb and index finger in left O, pull out, then slap right palm on left O.

Coke (Coca-Cola)
Hold left arm out. Stick upper arm with index finger of right L and wiggle thumb.

cocoa
Place thumb of right C (middle, fourth, and little fingers closed) on back of left hand and circle counterclockwise.

straw (drinking)
G shape both hands, tips facing. Place right G on left G then raise right G to mouth.

Practice signing and saying the following paragraphs. Finger-spell all words hyphenated letter by letter (e.g., m-o-t-h-e-r).

1. **Going on a Picnic**

   Let's go on a picnic t-o-d-a-y. Put paper plates, napkins, and a knife in this basket. We won't need any spoons o-r forks. I'm making chicken sandwiches with lettuce and mayonnaise. What kind o-f fruit would you like, grapes o-r apples? Let's take s-o-m-e salt and pepper with us. What should we have for dessert? We can have Coke t-o drink. Don't forget the straws; we aren't bringing glasses.

2. **Dinner Time**

   Please s-e-t the table for dinner. We'll need water glasses t-o-n-i-g-h-t. I've made spaghetti with meat sauce. Will you get mushrooms, tomatoes, and lettuce o-u-t o-f the refrigerator? This salad will taste better if we a-d-d more dressing. These pears with cheese will make a delicious dessert.

3. **Breakfast**

   Breakfast is my favorite m-e-a-l. In cold weather, I like t-o start o-f-f with a cup o-f hot cocoa. T-h-e-n comes my grapefruit! Next a plate o-f pancakes, sausage, and a lot o-f syrup. Of course, I a-l-s-o like bacon and eggs, toast and butter. I finish with a cup o-f black coffee.

4. **Snack Time**

   Do you want a snack before going o-u-t t-o play? You can have an apple with peanut butter o-n it. T-h-e-r-e are chocolate c-h-i-p cookies, t-o-o. Grandmother brought o-v-e-r a peach pie. That would be good with vanilla ice cream. I'm going t-o have some strawberries. H-e-r-e is your glass o-f milk. Be careful; don't spill it. Take the gum o-u-t o-f your mouth before you start eating.

11.
TRAVEL

INITIALIZED SIGNS

In American Sign Language one sign may stand for a number of different but related words. For example, the words *drive, car,* and *truck* may all use the same sign with slight variation in movement.

drive, car, truck

In English each of these words has a very different meaning—a car is not a truck; nor is the act of driving the same as the vehicle one drives. In order to be clear, in Signed English each word has its own unique sign.

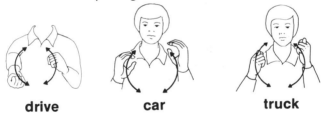

drive **car** **truck**

Drive is the base sign. When made with *c* handshapes, it becomes *car.* When made with *t* handshapes, it becomes truck. This process of developing new sign vocabulary by initializing a base sign is called "initialization."

Initialization is used extensively in Signed English to create much-needed sign vocabulary.

bicycle

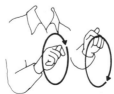

add T for tricycle

SIGNING ENGLISH WORD ORDER

In American Sign Language, one sign may represent an entire English sentence.

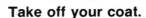

Take off your coat.

A person, seeing this sign, can easily understand what is being requested. However, the English language structure related to the request is not represented in the sign. By contrast, a user of Signed English forms a specific, distinct sign for each word in the sentence.

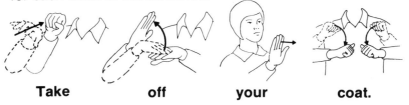

| **Take** | **off** | **your** | **coat.** |

Now the person sees a sign to represent each English word in sequence in the sentence. Other situational clues, such as a pile of coats on the bed or a hanger in the speaker's hand, can also assist in interpreting the meaning of the sentence.

By using Signed English, a person can change the pattern "take off your coat" to express new and different ideas.

> She is taking off her coat.
> I did not take off my coat.
> The man took off his coat.

SIGNING IDIOMS

Idioms are those odd phrases that make spoken and written English so varied, rich, and colorful. The meaning of an idiom is not understood by knowing the meaning of each word in the phrase. Instead, the meaning is determined by situational clues.

In Signed English, idioms are signed just as they are spoken. This process is called "literal signing."

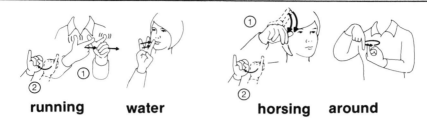

running   water   horsing   around

Literal signing helps language learners develop flexibility in their use of words. By pointing to the water coming from a faucet and then signing *running water*, the receiver understands that the word *run* does not always involve feet. This is exactly how a hearing child normally learns the multiple meanings of a word like *run*—by hearing the word used in a variety of situations. Perhaps the child will be told of "a run in a stocking" or find out a cat was "run over" by a car. The story on television may be about a child who "ran away" from home or a woman "running for president." By using the sign *run* each time in the above conversations, the receiver begins to develop an appreciation for the idioms and multiple word meanings found in abundance in spoken and written English.

Note: Some people may associate the sign *run* primarily with body movement and feel uncomfortable using it in a phrase such as "run for president." In such cases, the word *run* can be fingerspelled. You may fingerspell any word whose sign seems too iconic for general use.

SIGNING OPPOSITES

Certain pairs of signs having opposite meanings are very similar in handshape but have reverse movements. They tend to be iconic and easy to remember.

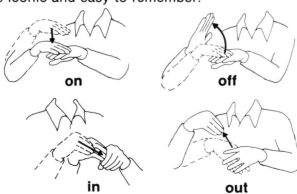

on   off

in   out

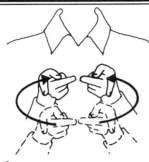

place
P shape both hands. Touch tips of middle fingers, circle back to body, and touch again.

rest room
R shape RH palm down. Bounce to right.

restaurant
R shape RH palm left. Place on right side of mouth then move to left side.

office
O shape both hands, tips out. Move right O left and left O right, indicating square shape.

store (noun)
Flat O shape both hands, tips down. Swing out twice.

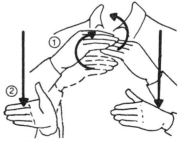

building
Open B both hands, palms down, tips facing. Alternately place one on top of other, moving upward. Then form sides of building, palms facing.

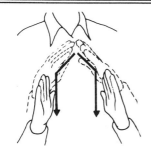

house

Place tips of both hands together to form roof. Move apart and down to form sides of house.

home

Place tips of right flat O to edge of mouth and move to upper cheek. (Sometimes made with right flat O moving to open B on cheek.)

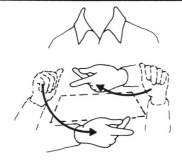

apartment

A shape both hands. Change into P shapes and bring left P behind right P, outlining shape of room.

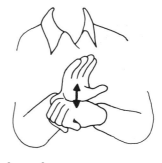

church

Tap right C on back of left S twice.

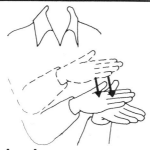

school

Open B both hands, left palm up, tips out; right palm down, tips left. Clap hands twice.

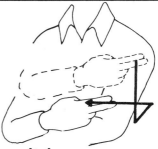

hospital

H shape RH. Make cross on upper left arm.

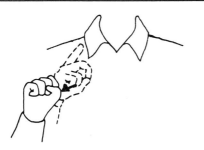

drugstore

Fingerspell D-S in quick succession. (A compound of *drug* and *store* may also be used.)

post office

Fingerspell P-O.

library

L shape RH. Circle in front of body.

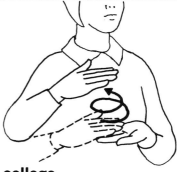

college

Clap hands together once then circle RH upward over left palm.

movie

Five shape LH palm right, tips out. Five shape RH palm left, tips up. Place palms together then gently shake right fingertips back and forth (to indicate flickering motion).

park

Open B shape LH palm down, tips out. P shape RH palm down. Circle right P over left arm up to elbow and back.

prison

Five shape both hands, palms in, right tips up, left tips right. Slap back of right fingers against left palm.

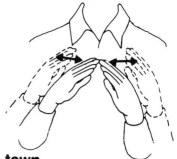

town

Open B both hands, palms facing, tips up. Tap tips together (indicating roofs of many buildings).

country

Rub left elbow clockwise with palm of right open B.

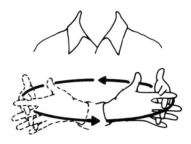

America

Interlock fingers, palms in, and circle from right to left.

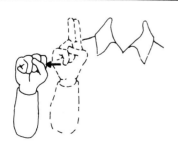

United States

Fingerspell U-S in quick succession as if one movement.

world

W shape both hands, tips out. Place right W on top of left. Circle right W forward and under left W, returning to original position.

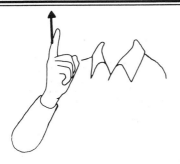

up
Point index finger up.

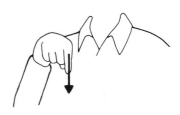

down
Point index finger down.

upstairs
One shape RH. Move up in two short movements.

downstairs
Point index finger down and move up and down twice.

on
Open B both hands, palms down, left tips out, right tips left. Place right palm on back of left palm.

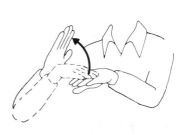

off
Open B both hands, palms down. Place right palm on back of left hand and lift off.

to

One shape both hands. Direct right
index toward left and touch. (Note:
As part of an infinitive, *to* is often
fingerspelled.)

until

One shape both hands. Arc tip of
right index over to tip of left index.

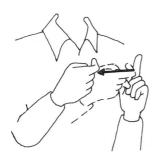

from

One shape LH palm right. Place
index finger of right X against left
index and draw back.

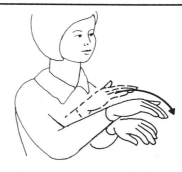

over

Open B both hands, palms down.
Pass RH over LH without touching.

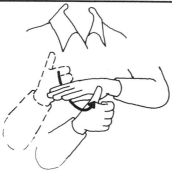

under

LH open B palm down. Pass right
A, thumb extended, under left
palm.

at

Touch back of left A with right
fingertips.

around
One shape LH palm in. Circle with right index which is held tip down.

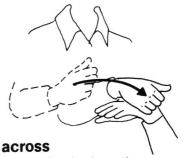

across
LH open B palm down, tips slanted right. Slide little finger edge of right A across back of LH.

between
LH open B palm and tips slanted right. Place little finger edge of right open B between left thumb and index and move back and forth.

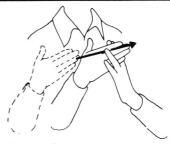

through
Five shape LH, open B shape RH. Pass right tips outward through left middle and fourth fingers.

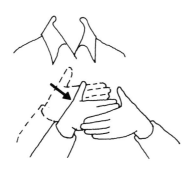

near
Open B both hands, palms in, thumbs up. Place back of right hand against palm of left.

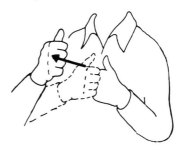

far
A shape both hands, thumbs up. Place right on back of left then move right A forward and out.

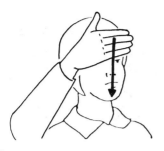

front

RH open B palm in, tips left. Hold in front of forehead then drop in front of face.

behind

A shape both hands, knuckles facing, thumbs up. Place knuckles together and draw RH in back of LH.

top

B shape both hands, left palm right, tips up; right palm down, tips left. Rest right palm on left tips.

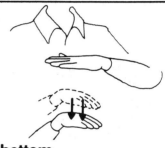

bottom

B shape both hands, palms down, left tips out, right tips left. Gently bounce right B under left B.

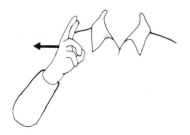

right (direction)

R shape RH. Move to right.

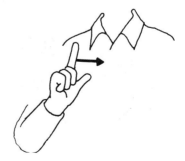

left (direction)

L shape RH palm out. Move from right to left.

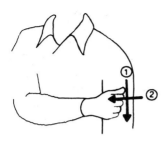

ambulance
Make cross on upper left arm with right A.

car
C shape both hands. Mime holding and turning steering wheel.

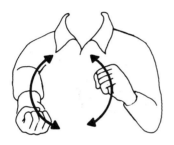

drive
A shape both hands. Move as if turning steering wheel of car. (Sometimes made with two D shapes.)

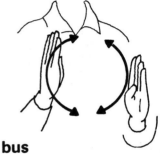

bus
B shape both hands, palms facing. Mime holding steering wheel and turning.

truck
Mime holding and moving steering wheel with T shape hands, palms facing.

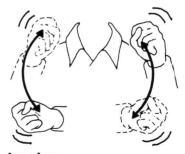

tractor
S shape both hands. Mime holding large steering wheel and turn in bouncy motions.

boat
Place little finger sides of open hands together, tips out, to form shape of boat. Move forward twice.

ship
LH open B palm up, tips out. Place right 3 in left palm and move forward twice.

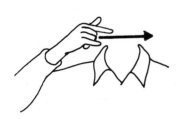

airplane
Y shape RH, index finger extended. Zoom to left.

helicopter
Support open right palm with left index finger and shake right fingers.

bicycle
S shape both hands, knuckles down, LH below RH. Circle up and down as if pedaling.

motorcycle
Hold S shape hands in front of body as if grasping large handlebars. Twist inward twice.

wheel
W shape RH palm left, tips out. Rotate outward in circular motion.

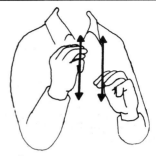

motor
M shape both hands, palms down, right tips left, left tips right. Place right M behind left then move hands up and down alternately.

train (noun)
H shape both hands, palms down, left tips out, right tips left. Rub right H back and forth on left H.

spaceship
H shape RH palm in, tips left, thumb extended. Bend finger and move swiftly to the left.

trip (noun)
RH bent V. Move forward in circular motion.

traffic
Five shape both hands. Place hands together and move back and forth alternately in rapid succession.

Practice signing and saying the following paragraphs. Finger-spell all words hyphenated letter by letter (e.g., m-o-t-h-e-r).

1. J-o-h-n thinks the United States is the best country in the world. Its libraries, parks, and restaurants are open to everyone. The stores are full o-f things t-o buy. Americans have beautiful houses and apartments. All o-f their children go to school and many a-t-t-e-n-d college. If people want t-o take a vacation outside o-f the country, they can. No one will throw them in prison for asking!

2. My s-o-n loves anything with wheels o-r a motor. His favorite machines are cars and trucks, followed b-y airplanes and helicopters. He jumps on his bicycle and pretends it's a motorcycle. If an ambulance o-r fire truck goes b-y the house, he runs to the front door and screams! Are all children like that?

3. A woman was hit b-y a c-i-t-y bus. She was taken by ambulance to the hospital emergency room. The accident happened near her office building. She was running across the street without looking. The driver o-f the bus couldn't stop in time. I saw it all from my upstairs bedroom window.

4. I'm new in town. Can you tell me where the post office is? Someone said it was between the drugstore and the college library. Could that small building across the street be it, the one near the church? I've looked all over the place for it.

12.
TIME, MONEY, SHAPES, and ADVERBS

DAYS OF THE WEEK

The days of the week are signed by forming the first letter(s) of the word with the right hand, then moving it in a small clockwise circle.

M for Monday

T for Tuesday

W for Wednesday

T-H for Thursday

F for Friday

S for Saturday

Sunday is an exception to the rule; it has its own special sign.

Sunday

Open B both hands,
palms out. Circle away
from each other.

MONTHS OF THE YEAR

The months of the year are fingerspelled just as they are written in complete or abbreviated form.

J-a-n	= January	J-u-l-y	= July
F-e-b	= February	A-u-g	= August
M-a-r-c-h	= March	S-e-p-t	= September
A-p-r-i-l	= April	O-c-t	= October
M-a-y	= May	N-o-v	= November
J-u-n-e	= June	D-e-c	= December

MONEY

Sign amounts of money as they are spoken.

fifty   **cents**   **= fifty cents (50¢)**

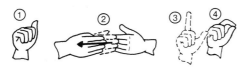

a   dollar   twenty   = a dollar twenty ($1.20)

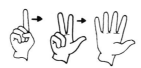

one - thirty - five   = one-thirty-five ($1.35)

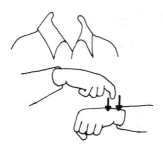

time
Tap back of left wrist with right index finger which is slightly bent.

before
Open B both hands, palms in, thumbs up. Place RH against left palm then move RH back toward body.

after
Open B both hands, palms in, left tips right, right tips left. Place right B on back of left. Turn out, ending with palm up.

already
Five shape RH palm in and slightly to the right. Twist out so that palm faces out.

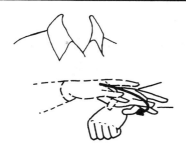

early
S shape LH palm down, knuckles out. Place tip of right middle finger on back of left S, bend down and over.

late
Hold right open B down by side. Wave back and forth twice.

next
Open B both hands, palms in. Place back of right fingers against left palm then arc RH over LH.

last (adj. & adv.)
I shape LH tip out. Strike down tip of left little finger with right index.

clock
Touch back of left wrist with right index finger. Then outline clock with double C shapes facing each other.

minute
LH open B palm right, tips up. Place knuckles of right 1 shape against left palm and move forward, ending with right index tip out.

hour
LH open B palm right, tips up. Place thumb knuckle of 1 shape RH against left palm and make a circle.

second (unit of time)
LH open B palm right, tips up. Place right thumb knuckle against left palm and move back and forth in small movements.

179

morning
Hold right hand out palm up. Place little finger side of left open B on inside of right elbow. Raise right arm to vertical position.

noon
Hold right arm straight up palm left, open B shape. Rest elbow on left open B palm down, tips right.

afternoon
Hold left arm before you, palm down, tips right. Place elbow of right open B on back of LH and lower slightly.

night
Hold left arm in front of body, palm and tips slanted down. Place heel of right open B, tips down, on left wrist.

yesterday
Place thumb of right A on right cheek. Arc back and touch back of cheek near ear. (Sometimes made with Y handshape.)

today
Drop cupped hands in front of body with palms up. Then rest elbow of right D on back of LH which is held across front of body. Arc thumb and index of right D down to inside of left elbow.

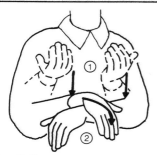

tonight

Drop cupped hands, palms up, in front of body. Then, with hands cupped palms down, drop RH down over left wrist.

tomorrow

A shape RH. Place thumb side on right cheek and arc forward.

calendar

LH open B palm in. C shape RH palm and tips left. Place RH in left palm then slide over tips and down back of LH.

day

Hold left arm before you palm down, tips right. Point right index finger up. Then rest right elbow on back of left hand and arc down to elbow.

week

LH open B palm up, tips out. One shape RH palm down, tip left. Slide RH across left palm from base to tip.

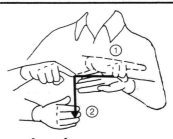

weekend

Slide palm of 1 shape RH, tip left, across left palm then drop down into open B.

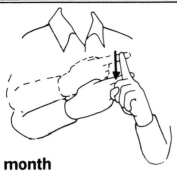

month
One shape both hands, left palm right; right palm in, tip left. Place right index against left and slide down.

year
S shape both hands. Place right S on top of left. Circle right S forward and under left S, ending in original position.

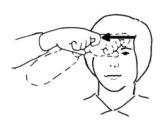

summer
X shape RH palm down, knuckles left. Draw across forehead from left to right

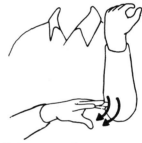

fall (season)
Hold left arm upright, palm in. Brush index finger of right open B (palm down, tips left) against left elbow.

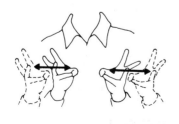

winter
W shape both hands, palms facing, tips out. Press upper arms against body, then shake hands back and forth in shivering motion.

spring (season)
Push right flat O up through left C, opening into 5 shape. Repeat motion.

never
B shape RH palm left, slanted up. Slash downward sharply, tips forming question mark shape.

not
A shape RH knuckles left, thumb extended. Place thumb under chin and move out.

yet
Hold Y shape RH palm in, tips down, near waist. Flap backward twice.

very
V shape both hands, palms facing. Place tips together and draw apart.

only
Hold right index finger up, palm out. Then twist, ending with palm in.

again
LH open B palm up, tips out. RH bent B palm up. Arc RH left and place tips in left palm.

away
RH open B palm in, tips left. Flip away and out.

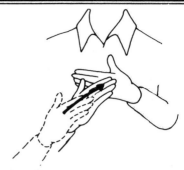

back
LH open B palm in, tips right. Touch back of LH with tips of right curved B.

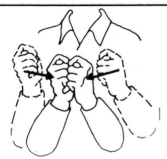

together
T shape both hands, thumbs out. Bring together.

too (in excess)
Bent open B both hands, palms down. Place right fingertips on left then arc RH upward.

too (also)
One shape both hands, palms down, tips out. Tap sides of index fingers together twice.

still
Y shape RH palm down. Arc down then up, ending with palm out.

sure
One shape RH palm left. Place index finger on mouth then move forward.

just (only)
LH open B palm right, tips up. Trace J on left palm with right little finger.

soon
LH open B palm right, tips up. Place side of right S in left palm and make a one-quarter turn forward.

almost
LH open B palm up, tips slightly right. Stroke back of left fingers with right fingers, bringing RH above LH.

always
One shape RH palm left, tip out. Circle continuously.

ever
E shape RH. Circle clockwise.

else
E shape RH knuckles left. Twist wrist so that knuckles face up.

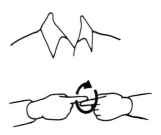

about
Point left index finger right, palm in. Circle with right index.

maybe
Open B both hands, palms up, tips out. Move up and down alternately.

then
L shape LH thumb up, index tip out. Place right index behind left thumb then move to tip of left index.

such
S shape both hands, knuckles out, index fingers touching. Draw up and apart.

much
Claw shape both hands, palms facing. Place tips close together then arc apart.

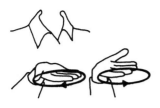

here

Open B both hands, palms up, tips out. Circle horizontally in opposite directions.

there

Point index finger out.

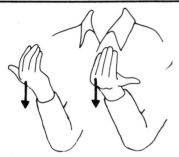

now

Bent open B both hands, palms up. Lower slightly.

later

L shape RH palm left, index tip up. Move up and forward in semi-circle.

sometimes

LH open B palm right, tips out. Place right index tip in center of left palm and slowly strike upward. Repeat motion.

once

LH open B palm right, tips out. Place right index tip in middle of left palm and strike upward once.

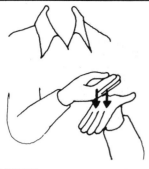

money

LH open B palm up, tips out. Tap left palm twice with back of right flat O.

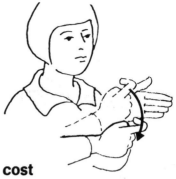

cost

LH open B palm right. Brush knuckle of right X down left palm.

change (money)

Arc right index back and forth on left index.

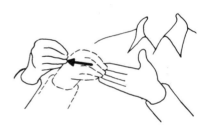

dollar

LH open B palm in, tips right. Grasp left fingers with right fingers and thumb. Draw RH back to right, ending in flat O shape.

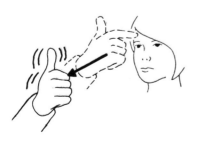

dime

Place right index finger on right temple. Bring out into 10 shape and shake.

nickel

Touch forehead with middle finger of right 5 then move hand out.

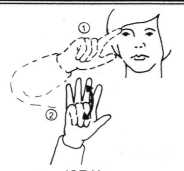

quarter (25¢)
L shape RH. Place index finger on forehead, move out and flutter last three fingers.

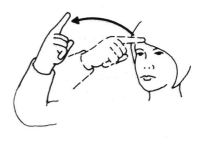

penny
Place right index on right temple then move hand out.

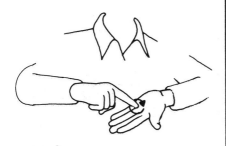

cent
Circle right index finger in left palm.

expensive
LH open B palm up. Place back of right flat O in left palm, lift up and out, then drop down, spreading fingers.

circle
C shape LH. Circle thumb side with right index finger clockwise. (Sometimes made without left C.)

round
C shape LH palm and tips out. R shape RH palm in, tips left. Circle left C with right R.

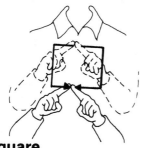

square

One shape both hands, palms out, index tips touching. Move apart, down, and back together, outlining shape of square. (Sometimes made with S handshapes.)

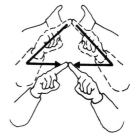

triangle

One shape both hands, palms out, tips touching. Outline shape of triangle. (Sometimes made with T handshapes.)

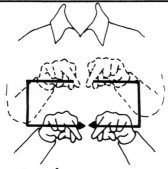

rectangle

R shape both hands, palms down, tips out. Outline shape of rectangle.

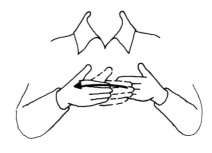

side

Open B both hands, palms in, left tips right, right tips left. Place RH on back of LH and slide to right.

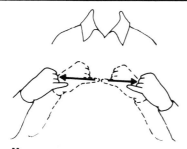

line

I shape both hands, palms in, tips touching. Draw apart in straight line.

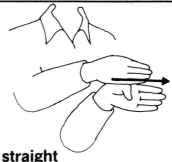

straight

B shape both hands, left palm right, right palm left, tips out. Move little finger side of right B straight out across index finger of left B.

Practice signing and saying the following paragraphs. Finger-spell all words hyphenated letter by letter (e.g., m-o-t-h-e-r).

1. It's very hard to believe that coffee now costs 50 cents a cup! I remember when you could buy a cup for a dime. It was that p-r-i-c-e for years. When it hit 15 cents, it soon went up to a quarter. Not much time p-a-s-s-e-d before it was 30 cents a cup and now—half a dollar. That's just too much money!

2. It's supposed t-o snow some time this weekend. However, I'm still going shopping on Saturday. Do you know why? I looked at my calendar this morning. There are only 8 days before Christmas. I have so much yet t-o buy! I'll never again wait until the last minute.

3. I saw T-o-m and S-u-e yesterday afternoon. They have planned a spring vacation in M-e-x-i-c-o. It's such a beautiful place t-o be in A-p-r-i-l. Of course, there is almost always a lot o-f rain that time o-f year. But, I'm sure everything else about the trip will be wonderful. Maybe we can go there later in the summer.

4. Mommy, do you know what we studied in school today? A rectangle has four sides. S-o does a square. A triangle is made o-f three straight lines. And guess what? A dollar is a rectangle. Pennies, nickels, dimes, and quarters are circles. Do you want me t-o draw all the different s-h-a-p-e-s on this paper?

GLOSSARY

American Sign Language: ASL, a "silent" visual-gestural language used by many deaf adults. It is often acquired as a first language by deaf children of deaf parents.

Amplification: Using a device to make sounds, including speech, louder. Hearing aids are a form of amplification.

Base (Basic) Sign: A sign that represents a base or root word, i.e., a word from which other words are formed. E.g., love is a root word; thus the sign for *love* is a base sign.

Compound: A single word which is made from two other words or signs. Usually the single word has a meaning similar to the meaning of the two words/signs. E.g., blue + berry = blueberry; now + day = today.

Deaf: Refers to people whose hearing losses are so severe that, even with the help of a hearing aid, they cannot clearly hear or understand speech.

Fingerspelling: Using a separate handshape for each letter of the English alphabet to spell out words. E.g., c-r-o-w, T-e-x-a-s.

Grammar: The structure, rules, and principles of a language.

Hearing-Impaired: Refers to people possessing various types of hearing losses, from very mild to severe.

Iconic: The way a sign resembles the word it represents. E.g., the sign for *cat* is iconic. It "paints a picture" of the cat's whiskers.

Idiom: A set phrase in a language, the meaning of which cannot be understood just by knowing the meaning of the individual words in the phrase. E.g., phrases such as "stood up" (on a date), "caught a bug" (became sick), "stuck up" (conceited) are English idioms.

Initialization:	A process of marking a basic ASL sign with manual alphabet hand configurations to produce new sign vocabulary. E.g., initialize the basic ASL sign for *much* with L handshapes to produce a new sign for *large*, G handshapes for *great*, B handshapes for *big*, etc.
Literal Signing:	Signing the exact English words in a phrase instead of the meaning behind the words. In Signed English, most idioms are signed literally. E.g., signing the idiom, "Cut that out!" would involve using the signs for *cut*, *that*, and *out*.
Manual:	Involving use of the hands. E.g., the manual alphabet is an alphabet formed on the hands.
Manual English:	Refers to any of the newly developed sign systems designed to represent English. Signed English is a form of Manual English.
Marker:	One of the "word parts" used in Signed English. The 14 markers are added to base signs to form new words. E.g., rain (base sign/word) + -y (marker) = rainy (new word)
Signed English:	A sign system which is intended to help its users develop English language structures. The signs reinforce the understanding, reading, and speaking of English. It is particularly beneficial for hearing parents who wish to share their English language heritage with their deaf children.
Syntax:	The way in which words are put together to form phrases and sentences.

REFERENCES

Bornstein, H. (1973). A description of some current sign systems designed to represent English. *American Annals of the Deaf, 118, 454-463.*

_____.(1974). Signed English: A manual approach to English language development. *Journal of Speech and Hearing Disorders, 39,* 330-343.

_____.(1990). *Manual communication: Implications for education.* Washington, DC: Gallaudet University Press.

_____.(1979). Systems of sign. In L. Bradford and W. Hardy (eds.) *Hearing and hearing impairment.* pp. 333-361). New York: Academic Press.

_____.(1982). Towards a theory of use for Signed English: From birth through adulthood. *American Annals of the Deaf, 127,* 26-31.

Bornstein, H., Saulnier, K., & Hamilton, L.B. (1980). Signed English: A first evaluation. *American Annals of the Deaf, 126,* 69-72.

Bornstein, H., & Saulnier, K. (1981). Signed English: A brief follow-up to the first evaluation. *American Annals of the Deaf, 126,* 69-72.

Rawlings, B. (1973). *Characteristics of hearing impaired students by hearing status,* U.S. 1970-71 (Series D., No. 10). Washington, D.C.: Gallaudet University Office of Demographic Studies.

Trybus, R., & Jensema, C. (1978). *Communication patterns and educational achievements of hearing impaired students* (Series T. No.2). Washington, D.C.: Gallaudet University Office of Demographic Studies

INDEX

INDEX

TITLES in the SIGNED ENGLISH SERIES

Beginning Books

Basic vocabulary, phrases, and simple sentences related to daily activities.

All by Myself

Baby's Animal Book

A Book about Me

Circus Time

Count and Color

Fire Fighter Brown

My Toy Book

The Pet Shop

Police Officer Jones

Growing Up Books and Stories

High interest-level topics presented in simple, straightforward sentences.

At Night: A First Book of
  Prepositions

The Clock Book

The Gingerbread Man

Goldilocks and the Three Bears

The Holiday Book

I Want to Be a Farmer

Little Lost Sally

Mealtime at the Zoo

Night/Day Work/Play

Spring is Green

The Three Little Kittens

The Ugly Duckling

More Stories and Poems

Advanced language patterns. Classic fairy tales, some with complicated plots and more sophisticated vocabulary.

Be Careful

Jack and the Beanstalk

Little Poems for Little People

Little Red Riding Hood

Mouse's Christmas Eve

The Night before Christmas

Nursery Rhymes from Mother Goose

Questions and More Questions

Songs in Signed English (with record)

The Three Little Pigs

We're Going to the Doctor

Reference Books

The Comprehensive Signed
  English Dictionary

The Signed English Starter

The Signed English Schoolbook

Signed English for the Classroom

Signed English for the Residence Hall

Flash Cards

Sign/Word Flash Cards

Coloring Books

Don't Be a Grumpy Bear

The Tale of Peter Rabbit

Posters

Jack and Jill

Manual Alphabet

Rock-a-Bye Baby